"A SUPERB piece of work. This is one of those rare books that is satisfying reading, interesting and educational. The prologue . . . manages to give a history of Russia that is excellent. And in the pages that follow, the author not only presents all that took place before and during the Communist Revolution, but also explains clearly: dialectic materialism, the philosophy of Marx, the difference between socialism and communism . . . to mention a few. Specially recommended."
—*Bestsellers*

"ROBERT GOLDSTON'S remarkable study of the Russian Revolution is brilliant. He fixes the setting in space, time, and history, analyzes the philosophical and political factors which underlay the conflict and describes the actual events of the uprising with eloquence and restraint.

"Goldston's synthesis of the Revolution's roots . . . could hardly be improved. Drawing liberally upon the vivid eyewitness accounts of John Reed and Nikolai Sukhanov, he recreates Petrograd during the Ten Days That Shook the World with great literary taste . . . .

"It is probably the best short summary on the Russian Revolution yet to be produced."
—Harrison Salisbury,
The New York Times Book Review

"THE AUTHOR'S vigorous, clearly written prose makes this history of the Russian Revolution an exceptional one among good ones."
—*Horn Book*

ROBERT GOLDSTON

THE RUSSIAN REVOLUTION

A FAWCETT PREMIER BOOK
Fawcett Publications, Inc., Greenwich, Conn.
Member of American Book Publishers Council, Inc.

For the Conroys—

past, present, and future

Acknowledgments

The author owes a debt of gratitude to the following publishers and authors for permission to quote, sometimes extensively, from the following copyrighted works: to International Publishers for permission to quote from *Ten Days That Shook the World*, by John Reed; to The University of Michigan Press for permission to quote from *The History of the Russian Revolution*, by Leon Trotsky, translated by Max Eastman; to Mr. Joel Carmichael for permission to quote from *The Russian Revolution*, by N. N. Sukhanov, translated and edited by Joel Carmichael; to Mr. Edmund Wilson for permission to quote from *To the Finland Station*, by Edmund Wilson.

Author's Note

Until a few weeks after the Bolshevik revolution, Russia held to the old Julian Calendar which by 1917 was running thirteen days behind the Gregorian Calendar in use throughout the rest of the civilized world. All the dates in this book have been corrected to the Gregorian Calendar which is presently in effect. On the other hand, it has seemed best to retain the names of events which have gone into Russian history under their original designations. Thus, the "February Revolution" is called just that, even though on the Gregorian Calendar it took place in March.

Contents

THE RUSSIAN
REVOLUTION

Eternal Russia

THERE IS, above all, a sense of great distances, of vast and desolate wastelands reaching past far horizons. The icy wind that howls through the broad boulevards of Moscow may have whistled four thousand miles over the frozen plains. Rising in the fastnesses of central Asia, it has found no barrier to block its force. Passing through the bleak valleys of the snow-capped Ural Mountains, which define but do not divide European from Asiatic Russia, it has raced over half-frozen rivers which wind a thousand miles to the Arctic

Ocean, visited great cities that rise abruptly from the plains, touched the edges of lakes so huge they are classified as inland seas, weathered the faces of millions of people. But mountains, rivers, cities, seas, people—all seem remote and isolated in the silent immensities of Russia. From Leningrad, Russia's "window on the west," to Vladivostok on the Sea of Japan, one-sixth of the land area of the globe is enclosed within the boundaries of The Union of Soviet Socialist Republics. The Arctic Ocean, the fog-bound waters of Alaska, the Great Wall of China, the Tibetan "roof of the world," the approaches to India, the blistered deserts of Persia, the intricate frontiers of Turkey, Romania, Hungary, Czechoslovakia, Poland, and Finland—all these are mere stretches of the border which defines this gigantic empire.

The very size of this great land mass has helped give it a terribly severe climate. The winters are long and bitterly cold—temperatures of thirty or forty degrees below zero are normal throughout most of the country. But Russians have grown used to preparing for these winters with all the grim determination of a military campaign. From the largest metropolitan hotels to the poorest farmer's cottage, double doors, double windows and thick drapes close out the icy cold. In most buildings huge Russian stoves—tall as a man and four feet wide—generally overheat the cramped interiors. City-dwellers go about in layers of clothing topped by fur coats and hats which give them the appearance of an army of bears.

Spring literally explodes in Russia with the cracking of the icebound rivers. Floods are common, and the roads become seas of mud into which farm animals have been known to sink out of sight. But within a matter of weeks the terribly hot, dry, and dusty Russian summer parches most of the land. The temperature soars so high that in parts of Siberia the farmers complain that the bare soil burns their feet. Two or three months of this excessive heat is relieved by a very short autumn; then comes the long, frigid winter again.

Some have seen in this climate the origins of the Russian character, which is supposed to consist of long periods of depressed laziness followed by sudden feverish bouts of gaiety and energy. All winter long the farmers hibernate and then burst into frantic activity during the short growing season. But the only certain effect of the climate upon the national character has been to make Russians very hardy. Foreigners never fail to be amazed at the sight of a sturdy Russian farm woman drawing water from a well with her bare hands while the thermometer registers forty degrees below zero. Both Napoleon and Hitler learned to their sorrow that it was not only the severity of the Russian winter but also the Russian ability to endure it which wrecked their dreams of empire.

The land is as harsh as its climate. Nearly half the soil of the USSR is permanently frozen beneath a surface depth of one foot; two thirds of the country is covered by endless forestland. An area as large as the eastern seaboard of the United States erupts in huge mountain masses, while burning deserts cover an area the size of all the trans-Mississippi West. Although it is almost three times the size of the United States, the Soviet Union has no greater area of arable land. Climate and the lack of arable land have combined to produce terrible famines in the past and chronic food shortages even today. But if the soil resists agriculture, it yields rich rewards of minerals, timber, and oil. Coal and iron as well as manganese (a key ingredient in steel) are plentiful. Hydro-electric power, drawn from such great rivers as the Don, the Volga, the Dnieper, and the Yenisei, supplies energy for the vast industrial complexes which make Russia the world's second largest industrial power. In the past these rivers provided the natural transportation routes for trade and migration; today their place has been taken by air, rail, and highway networks.

An ancient peasant proverb claims "Russia is not a country, it is a world." During the time of the czars Russia was called a "prison of nations." There are, in fact, over 170 different nationalities and more than 200 languages and dialects spoken in the Soviet Union. The principal groups in this population are the Russians, the White Russians (Russians with a heavy admixture of Polish and German blood, inhabiting the western border regions), and the Ukrainians. These Slavic peoples comprise more than 75 percent of the total population and are the core of the Russian state. Another large group, centered in mid-Asia, are the Turko-Mohammedan descendants of vanished Islamic empires. Farther to the east are scattered large seminomadic tribes of Mongols, Chinese, and Koreans. The German, Jewish, and Baltic peoples of Russia's western borderlands—who played such a large part in bringing Western thought and culture to the Slavs— have been scattered by war and government policy to distant corners of the Soviet Union, while the wild and colorful tribes of the Caucasus and the middle-eastern frontiers have been subdued and civilized. There are today fifteen Republics in the Union and many autonomous areas. While distinct national cultures and languages have been encouraged in these Republics, political power remains centered in Moscow.

The Slavic peoples of Russia entered late upon the stage of world history, and their development lagged hundreds of years behind that of the West. Not until six centuries after the fall of Rome—a thousand years after the birth of Christ—did a coherent civilization appear in Russia. This was the Federation of Kiev, a loosely organized region of the Ukraine dominated by the great city of Kiev on the banks of the river Dnieper. Its culture was derived from the Byzantine Empire, the successor to the Roman Empire in the Near East. From the imperial city of Byzantium (later Constantinople), Kievan traders brought back the arts, handcrafts, and Greek Orthodox Christianity, which were to mold Russian culture; even the Russian alphabet was based on the Greek. But with the fall of Constantinople to the Crusaders in the early thirteenth century, and with the rising pressures of internal dissension, the Kievan civilization decayed. No longer able to defend themselves against the raids of barbaric nomad tribes from the East, the peasants, traders, and princes of Kiev began to migrate to the safety of the northern forests. There they came under the domination of the Princes of Muscovy, semibarbaric hereditary rulers of the area around Moscow, which was then little more than a collection of wooden huts.

In 1237 complete and overwhelming disaster fell upon the Russian land; vast Mongol armies under the brilliant leadership of Batu Khan (a descendant of Genghis) invaded and conquered the plains, sweeping everything before them to the gates of Vienna. Slaughtering the entire populations of various areas along their way, deporting whole races, the Mongols fastened a grip upon Russia which was to last for centuries. The entire central and southern portion of the country fell to the Tatars. Kiev was burned to the ground, Moscow and other cities enslaved. Skilled craftsmen were carried off to the Mongol capital of Sarai in central Asia, trade came to a standstill, and crushing taxes were imposed on the starving peasants. While the Dark Ages gave way to a renaissance in western Europe, Russia

17

struggled to emerge from the Mongol domination. The Khans saw no need to station troops in Russia; the terror of their name was sufficient to ensure obedience. Instead they appointed certain petty Russian princes to collect the taxes and slaves for them. Among these princes the Princes of Muscovy eventually won the right to be sole tax collectors for the Great Khan. Every year they sent caravans of Russian slaves and gold and timber to the south, to the fabled lands of the Golden Horde, which stretched from the Ukraine to Turkestan.

Using the threat of the Mongol terror, the Princes of Muscovy made the Russian Orthodox Church into a servile branch of government. Slowly but surely they wiped out the petty independent principalities of northern Russia. Where the Princes of Muscovy's power extended, the peasants, the nobility (*boyars*) and the small merchants and traders were crushed and enslaved. But the Princes of Muscovy were careful not to rouse the anger of the Great Khan in the East as they slowly gathered strength and bided their time. By 1480 the power of the Golden Horde had fallen so low, while that of the Princes of Muscovy had risen so high, that they felt free to defy the Khan, refuse to pay further taxes, and so end three centuries of foreign domination.

This slow conquest of northern Russia by the Princes of Muscovy, their continual subversion of the Mongol power, was accomplished at a terrible price. The nobility had been impoverished and reduced to complete dependence on the Princes; the Orthodox Church existed only on their sufferance. The peasants, living always on the edge of starvation, found their primitive liberties destroyed. By the beginning of the sixteenth century there was no power in all the broad land of Russia save that of the Prince of Muscovy. His autocracy was absolute, with no group, no institution to gainsay his word. From this time until the late nineteenth century the history of Russia becomes very largely a personal history of the country's rulers. Behind the throne one is aware of vast, silent multitudes suffering; around the throne fawning courtiers sparkle momentarily and are then snuffed out. From time to time a general, a statesman, a poet makes his appearance. But Russia is the personal property of its ruler, the people his absolute slaves. Government policy, law, religion, life, and death all reflect the often-crazed personal whims of the inheritors of the Princes of Muscovy.

In 1533, Ivan IV became Prince of Muscovy. Fourteen years later he assumed the title of Czar (Caesar) of All the Russias. He is better known to history as Ivan the Terrible. He faced three problems which were to plague all his successors and which still have not been completely settled. First of all there was the constant need to organize, to centralize the vast and sprawling Russian domains. This was to be accomplished by making everyone—noble, priest, tradesman, and peasant—a servant of the state under rigid control. Second, Russia, without natural frontiers on the west and with barbaric tribes in the east, found itself ringed and threatened by enemies. These were to be crushed by constant war and the maintenance of huge armies. Third was the problem of the technological and cultural backwardness of the nation. This was to be solved by the large-scale importation of engineers, craftsmen, and advisors from the West.

Like most of his successors, Ivan found it much easier to smash the power of the decaying Mongol khanates in the East than to cope with the powerful armies of Poland and Sweden in the west. His reign was marked by constant warfare, desperate oppression, and savage cruelty. In this it was not remarkable. There has hardly been a czar in Russian history who would not have as well deserved to be named "the Terrible."

Under Ivan the Russian conquest of the Mongols was completed, and all the vast land of western Siberia annexed. But the exhaustion of this effort and the struggle for power which occurred when Ivan's son died without leaving an heir to the throne led to the Time of Troubles—of peasant uprisings and civil war —which lasted until a nobleman named Mikhail Romanov assumed the throne in 1613. His descendants were to rule for more than three hundred years in an unbroken line.

The Romanovs brought no new policy to the throne. They continued to increase the absolute autocracy they enjoyed, degrading all classes more and more. In 1649, Alexei Romanov produced a new legal code which divided and froze the Russian people into rigid classes. Peasants were bound to the land, townspeople to their town or city. The Church and nobility were declared closed classes, and both were strictly regulated by the Czar. Thus, at a time when feudalism had almost disappeared in the West, something very much like it was formally codified and frozen into existence in Russia.

But if the czars were absolute at home, they remained apprehensive of foreign enemies. Recognizing that only by adopting Western technology could they hope to preserve their empire, the Romanovs now strove to modernize their nation. Peter I, remembered as Peter the Great, who ruled from 1682 to 1725, made a mighty effort to "westernize" his people. He issued regulations and laws which even went so far as to abolish beards and the old costume of the people. Importing engineers from Scotland, France, and England along with Italian architects, Peter built a vast and modern city on the shores of the Baltic Sea. Named in his honor Saint Petersburg, it was built by the brute force of untold thousands of serfs. It was said that every stone in the city represented the life of a worker.

When Peter died in 1725, some of his innovations died with him, but he left behind a legacy of hatred and chaos worthy of a Romanov.

Russia was now a great world power, and if its peasantry remained in illiterate slavery, its nobility made haste to copy Western tastes and culture. French became the fashionable language at Court (which Peter had moved to Saint Petersburg from Moscow), and the Russian people came to be regarded as animals by their newly educated masters.

After a brief repetition of the Time of Troubles, during which czars came and went (often murdered by members of their own families), peasant rebellions flared and died, and the nobility won back a measure of its independence. Catherine II (the Great) seized the throne from her insane husband in 1762. Although she liked to consider herself an enlightened ruler, she did nothing in actuality to relieve the misery of her people. A succession of her lovers, promoted to the rank of general, succeeded in conquering the Ukraine and the Crimea from the Turks and local tribesmen. (During one of these complicated wars against the Turks, John Paul Jones was hired to reorganize the Russian Black Sea fleet, a task he accomplished with much grumbling but great success.)

Catherine's foreign policy in the West led to the dismemberment and enslavement of Poland among Russia, Prussia, and Austria. The mistake of thus destroying the buffer kingdom between Russia and Germany was to cost Catherine's descendants dearly.

During these centuries of Romanov rule, while Russia remained a prison for its people, Russian influence in the rest of the world was steadily growing. It reached a peak under Catherine's grandson, Alexander I. It was during Alexander's reign that Napoleon launched his Grande Armée into the icy fastness of the Russian wilderness. The deadly winter, the guerrilla warfare of the peasants, the scorched-earth policy which culminated in the accidental burning of Moscow, and the valor of the Russian armies, led by the brilliant General Mikhail Kutuzov, utterly destroyed the French forces—and with them Napoleon's dream of world domination.

The hardy serfs, with their fierce Cossack cavalry, swept across Europe to join the British, Swedes, and Prussians in bringing Napoleon's empire to an end. Russian divisions marched down the Champs Élysées in Paris, while Russian diplomats now found themselves a great influence in the West.

But at this peak of imperial glory the Romanov power had reached its zenith. By exposing his army officers to Western ideas and ways of life, Alexander was undermining his own position. When he died suddenly in 1825, a group of these officers attempted to overthrow the autocracy in favor of a democratic, representative government. Known as the Decembrists because of the month in which they struck, they were quickly and efficiently crushed by the new czar, Nicholas I. It is unlikely they could have succeeded, in any event. The Decembrists had the backing of certain elements of the nobility, the army, and the landowners, but they were almost as far removed from the enslaved masses of the Russian peasants and workers as was the Czar. The Decembrists did succeed in throwing a scare into Nicholas, however. His answer to the uprising was to inflict thirty years of the most savage repression upon all classes of his people. Schools, newspapers, the army, and the Church all felt the heavy hand of an even tighter, even more ruthless repression than that which they had grown used to. Surprisingly, for reasons which have never been fully explained, these years of czarist terror saw the emergence of many great Russian writers. The poet Alexander Pushkin and novelists Nikolai Gogol, Ivan Turgenev, Feodor Dostoevsky, and Leo Tolstoy all flourished during this time.

In the realm of foreign affairs Nicholas' policies—mostly aimed at gaining control of Constantinople and the straits between the Black Sea and the Mediterranean—led to the humiliating defeat inflicted upon Russia by France and England in the Crimean War. It was this disaster which prompted Nicholas' successor to the throne, Alexander II, to institute a few long-overdue reforms.

Alexander II may have had some slight personal regret for the hideous conditions under which his people toiled, but his primary concern was with the technological and social backwardness that had led to defeat in the Crimea. He traced these conditions to the existence of serfdom. The tiny but growing class of capitalist manufacturers agreed that free labor might be more efficient than slave labor. For these reasons, in 1861, Alexander abolished serfdom throughout Russia. But instead of giving the land to the peasants, much of it was sold to the rich while the rest was declared to be communal land—state property. This half-measure only enraged the peasants, who soon found themselves sunk in a morass of debt not much better than their former slavery. Reforms in the universities, the press, the judicial system, the army, and the local governments followed—all designed not to help the people so much as to make the government more efficient. But where there had been individual voices raised against the czar in the past, where leaderless peasants had erupted into savage but local uprisings, where officers or nobility had conspired in small, isolated plots, Alexander's Russia had for too long been exposed to Western political and social ideas. He faced, in the declining years of his life, a widespread and vocal opposition. Revolutionary plots against the government made Alexander a hunted man in his own empire. On March 13, 1881, the revolutionary discontent which had been gathering strength in Russia for untold centuries caught up with Alexander II. He was blown up by a bomb tossed at him as he drove in his carriage through Saint Petersburg.

Now the czardom was face to face with the masses of the people. It did not matter that the bomb-throwers were a tiny group of intellectuals; they were acting in conscious support of the wrath of peasants and workers, who wanted a program of social and economic as well as political reform. Alexander III, who was a horrified witness of his father's death, might indulge in an orgy of revenge and repression. Statutes, laws, decrees —each more reactionary than the ones before—might flow in a flood from Saint Petersburg. But the great mass of the Russian people were in motion at last. After centuries of oppression, after being treated like beasts for a thousand years, deep tides were stirring among workers and peasants. Czars, courtiers, generals, nobility, and priests might speak fondly of "Eternal Russia"—the never-changing empire of ignorance and oppression, the vast bulwark of tradition and obedience—but they were in the twilight of their power. Against them the rising tide of mass hatred was ready to break and it was armed with that most terrible of weapons—an idea, an idea forged by a handful of lonely scholars in the West which was destined to destroy the Romanovs and shake the world.

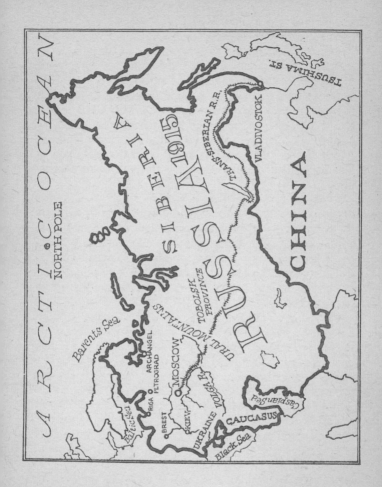

CHAPTER ONE

The Rise of Marxism

LIKE ALL SYSTEMS of ideas, Marxism was a long time developing. It did not spring entirely from the mind of the man whose name it bears, nor was it a scheme devised to be forced upon an unwilling world by a small band of conspirators. It was and remains a flawed but very useful view of the world and man's place in it. Like any system of thought which pretends to be universal, it has many inconsistencies; many of its prophecies have never come to pass, many of its analyses are demonstrably false. Marxism has been used and abused as a sort of intellectual bludgeon by radicals, while to conservatives it has become something of a bogey. Nevertheless, many of its views of history, many of its principles are a permanent part of the intellectual heritage of all men. It is primarily a system of analysis—a key among others for the unlocking of some of the mysteries of man's behavior. If this key fails to fit many locks, it remains nonetheless useful when properly employed. There are today no serious statesmen, economists, or historians anywhere in the world, no matter how conservative, who do not make use of it in one way or another.

Karl Marx was born in 1818 in the German city of Trier, close to the French border. His ancestors had for generations been studious and deeply respected rabbis in the Jewish community of that city—a heritage Marx himself was to disregard and discard. But the tremendous moral force of his work and life (as well as the self-righteous intolerance with which he treated those who disagreed with him) made him seem very close to those Old Testament prophets whose teachings he would have been the first to deride. He was a brilliant scholar, recognized as a genius by his teachers while still a student. In 1835 he went to the University of Bonn. There his activities, which included the usual (at that time) student drunkenness, rowdyism, and even dueling, made his father decide to transfer him to the University of Berlin. There he was to study law—but he actually studied philosophy. He devoted himself tirelessly to his studies, consuming books at a great rate and groping toward ideas which were to be his life's work.

Like all great thinkers, Marx was profoundly influenced by his age and the ideas which dominated it. Only by examining the intellectual climate of Marx' times can we discover the origins of his thought and the reasons for its still-potent vitality.

The basic terms of Marxism—that man is a rational animal, that the world he inhabits is a natural world which can be understood by his senses rationally applied, that man's history is the work of man himself, that this history can therefore be understood and even controlled—were the fruit of the centuries-long struggle of the modern world to emerge from the Dark Ages. The Renaissance had seen the rebirth of secular learning and thought after the long night which followed the downfall of Rome; the Reformation had struck from man's mind many of the shackles of superstition, while the growth of an inductive scientific outlook had placed at his disposal both a new understanding of his environment and new powers with which to organize it. The feudal organization of society which had been naturally appropriate to earlier ages was now crumbling under the assault of the new scientific philosophy, the skeptical spirit of rationalism, and, above all, the rapid growth of new means of production and distribution. The eighteenth century had seen the steady intensification of this assault: Voltaire mocking the old gods out of existence; Condorcet and Diderot erecting human intelligence itself as the new God; Rousseau discovering the virtues of "natural man"— these were some of the more notable gravediggers of the old order.

In the newly developing colonies of North America such men as Thomas Paine, Thomas Jefferson, Benjamin Franklin, and the Adamses were busily throwing off the last remnants of the past and organizing a new society to be based as much as humanly possible on the conscious application of human reason. The very fact that these men believed their new society could emerge from such written and reasonably organized documents as the Constitution and the Bill of Rights was in itself revolutionary.

There had been speculative attempts before to provide a theoretically rational basis for society. Sir Thomas More had published his book *Utopia* as early as 1516, and even the ancients, notably Aristotle and Plato, had tried their hands at planning theoretically perfect human societies. But their efforts had been crippled by lack of scientific knowledge, by superstition, and above all by their expectation of supernatural intervention in human affairs. The new social philosophers, both in America and in the Old World, were attempting to apply scientific principles to the study of human behavior. As early as 1725 an obscure Italian scholar named Giovanni Vico had written, "Governments must be conformable to the nature of the governed; governments are even a result of that nature."

Then in 1789 occurred an event which was to ignite into flame all the theories, all the ideals of isolated thinkers—the French Revolution. The vast masses of peasants and workers throughout France, and especially in Paris, with one huge convulsive shrug shook off the slavery of feudalism and routed the ancient monarchy which had oppressed them for generations. A new world seemed about to be born, a world of *Liberté, Égalité, Fraternité.* But very quickly a paradox developed—a paradox which was to lead to the rise of socialist theory. The Revolution, which had been won by the masses of the poor, had been led by the middle classes. It was they who roused the people to destroy the ancient regime. The monarchy's interference with their newly developing manufacturing, its suppression of their civil rights, its corruption, and its feudal control of the land made it as hated by the middle classes as by the poor. But once middle-class aims had been achieved, the Revolution was supposed to end. Yet to the propertyless, landless masses of the people, middle-class aims were not enough. They had not spilled their blood merely to substitute a new set of masters for the old ones. And now they were in control. Revolutionary terror descended over Paris and the provinces. Madame Guillotine claimed her victims by the thousand. The entire idea of private property, of a government designed to protect private property, came more and more under attack as the masses remained poor and starving in spite of the Revolution. Thus the middle classes found themselves now driven to undermine and suppress the very revolution they had led. A Directory was established, consisting of men who would respect property rights and put an end to the terror. Exhausted by years of struggle and bloodshed, the peasants and workers found themselves deprived of many of their hard-won rights. A new constitution was devised—so reactionary that the exiled monarchists announced it would suit them very well if only there was a king. Within a short time this new reaction was to lead to the dictatorship of Napoleon. But before that happened, one last and, for our purposes, extremely important gasp was to be heard from the masses.

In 1795 a man named François Noël Babeuf denounced the Directory. The Directory had restricted voting rights, he declared, and had speculated in gold while the poor starved on the streets of Paris. He demanded both political and, most terrifying of all, economic equality. Jailed and persecuted by the police, Babeuf founded an organization called the Society of Equals. This group demanded that there should be "no more individual property in land; the land belongs to no one. . . . We declare that we can no longer endure, with the enormous majority of men, labor and sweat in the service and for the benefit of a small minority." Driven underground by the police, the Society of Equals plotted a new uprising against the Directory. When they achieved power, there was to be a great national community of goods, equal education for all, work as a duty for all—and the necessities of life were to be supplied by the government. In demanding these reforms, they said, they were asking no more than the Revolution had promised. But the revolutionary excitement of the masses was now exhausted. Whatever energy the people had left was being siphoned off into Napoleon's victories in Italy in 1796. The Society of Equals was betrayed by a spy, its members arrested, and Babeuf himself carted off in a cage. His defense before the court was a passionate and closely reasoned apology for what later came to be recognized as socialist aims and ideals—the first such coherent statement before history.

The cause of revolutions, Babeuf told his judges, was the bending beyond what they could bear of the human springs of society. The people eventually rebel against this pressure and in so doing they are right, because the aim of society must be the greatest good for the greatest number. Happiness in Europe is a new idea, he said, but today we realize that the unhappy are the really important powers of this earth. In prosecuting him, Babeuf pointed out, the court was really prosecuting the philosophers of the Revolution itself. Had not Rousseau, for instance, spoken of "men so odious as to dare to have more than enough while other men are dying of hunger"? And Mably had declared, "If you follow the chain of our vices you will find that the first link is fastened to the inequality of wealth."

Babeuf's view of society was not merely theoretical. Remaining poor all his life, he had seen his seven-year-old daughter starve to death during the time of famine while the Republican middle classes speculated in gold.

After a six-day defense (marked by great dignity) Babeuf concluded by saying that the death sentence would not surprise or frighten him. He had gotten used to violence over the years—and, of course, the middle-class Republic was much harsher than the monarchy had ever been to its political enemies. Turning at last to his family, seated in the gallery of the courtroom, he said:

> But, oh, my children . . . I have but one bitter regret to express to you: that, although I have wanted so much to leave you a heritage of liberty which is the source of every good, I foresee in the future only slavery, and that I am leaving you a prey to every ill.
>
> I have nothing at all to give you! I would not even leave you my civic virtues, my profound hatred of tyranny, my ardent devotion to the cause of Liberty and Equality, my passionate love of the People. I would be making you too disastrous a gift! What would you do with it under the monarchic oppression which is certainly going to descend on you? I am leaving you slaves, and it is this thought alone which will torture my soul in its final moments. I should equip you for this situation with advice as to how to bear your chains more patiently, but I do not feel I am capable of it.

On May 27, 1796, Babeuf went to the guillotine. From prison he wrote to a friend, "I believe that in some future day men will give thought again to the means of procuring for the human race the happiness we have proposed for it."

Perhaps even more important than Babeuf's theoretical analyses and predictions was the terrible moral force behind him and his words. It is the outrage at injustice, the sympathy with the poor and starving which command our emotions as well as our attention. This is a quality which, while also one of the most powerful elements of Marxist persuasion, is common to all thinking men since the days of the French Revolution and before.

Very different from Babeuf in birth and background, but sharing his moral passion for the betterment of mankind, was Claude-Henri de Rouvroy, Comte de Saint-Simon. Born of one of the oldest and most aristocratic families of France, Saint-Simon had adopted republican principles early in life. Like his better-known aristocratic friend Lafayette, he had journeyed to America and fought on the side of the colonies in the American Revolution. But, perhaps from his experience of war and bloodshed during that struggle, he stood aloof from the French Revolution when it came, feeling that it was mainly a work of destruction. There seems little doubt that Saint-Simon was more than slightly mad. He had been imprisoned as an aristocrat during the time of revolutionary terror in Paris and he imagined that his great ancestor, the Emperor Charlemagne, visited him in his cell to urge him to become a philosopher. After his release from prison he set about to follow this advice, systematically learning physics, mathematics, medicine, and foreign languages. From his study of history Saint-Simon concluded that just as science had its laws, so human society was governed by laws. Furthermore, these laws were essentially economic. The principal object of any society was the organization of economic production and distribution. Also, the dream of individual liberty was simply irrelevant to social problems. Society as a whole must always take precedence over any of its parts. Government, according to Saint-Simon, was to be organized on the basis of a new aristocracy of intellect and merit, with the most intelligent joined into a supreme ruling council. He gave this council the name "The Council of Newton" because he had a vision in which God informed him that Newton was to replace the Pope as God's voice on earth.

Saint-Simon wrote prodigiously, and since no one could be found to publish him, he printed and distributed his books at his own expense. This soon brought him to poverty, and his last years were spent in misery. In his last book, *The New Christianity,* Saint-Simon, while retaining his principle of organizing society on aristocratic principles, indicated that if the rich and powerful of this world would not see that the betterment of the masses was in their own best interests, it would be necessary to organize those masses to act for themselves. "Princes!" he wrote, ". . . throw off the belief that the hired armies, the nobility, the heretical clergy, the corrupt judges, constitute your principal supporters . . . remember that Christianity commands [Princes] to devote their energies to bettering as rapidly as possible the lot of the very poor!"

Saint-Simon himself was now one of those "very poor." In 1823 he tried to shoot himself but failed. In 1825 he died in abject poverty.

While Saint-Simon called on the world to organize itself according to his revelations, a slightly more reasonable but hardly less visionary scheme of social organization was urged by Charles Fourier. Like Saint-Simon a victim and passive enemy of the French Revolution, Fourier had personally witnessed some of the paradoxes and horrors of the Industrial Revolution in France. He had once watched a cargo of rice being dumped into the harbor at Marseilles by his employers for the purpose of keeping the price of rice high, although the city was in the grip of a famine at the time.

Fourier, like Saint-Simon a victim of visions and revelations, believed that if he could organize small, self-contained societies in France based on his own views of human needs and abilities, it would be only a matter of time before all mankind would recognize the excellence of these societies and imitate them on a universal scale.

Fourier believed that human emotions, abilities, and ambitions had been given man by God. It was simply a matter of organizing men so that each faculty was put to constructive use. Fourier counted on financing his communities by donations from the rich. And, although there was to be universal suffrage, equal education for all, and an equal obligation upon everyone to work, there were to be some differences of income. Unpleasant work was to be more highly paid, and income was to be distributed by a system of dividends in which capital, labor, and talent shared almost equally, with labor drawing the largest dividends.

Fourier announced to the world that he would be at home every day at noon, fully prepared to discuss his schemes with any capitalists who might be interested in putting up the money for them. But although he waited at noon every day for ten years, no one came forward. He died in 1837 disappointed but not disillusioned.

While Fourier was carefully organizing human passions into a theoretical system and awaiting a patron who would enable him to test his schemes, an Englishman named Robert Owen had proceeded in a much more practical manner. Born in 1771, Robert Owen left home at the age of ten to work in the cotton mills of Manchester. So successful was he that by the time he was twenty, he was in charge of an entire factory. From that position he had ample opportunity to see the misery and degradation into which the factory workers were plunged by the greed of the owners.

More than that, he also saw that the constant cheating, exploitation, and bickering of the factory owners debased them almost as much as it debased the workers. Of the capitalist system of his day Owen wrote: "Under this system, there can be no true civilization; for by it all are trained civilly to oppose and often to destroy one another by their created opposition of interests. It is a low, vulgar, ignorant, and inferior mode of conducting the affairs of society. . . ."

Purchasing an interest in the cotton mills at New Lanark in Scotland, Robert Owen attempted to put some of his ideas into practice. He found the factory workers on his arrival to be thoroughly demoralized, drunken, thieving, and unreliable, but by limiting working hours, increasing salaries, improving their living conditions, and establishing a health and savings fund for the workers, he gradually fostered in them a growing self-respect which, in a very short time, made both mills and workers the envy of his competitors. In his journal *The New Moral World,* Owen had written: "Any general character, from the best to the worst . . . may be given to any community . . . by the application of proper means." The success of New Lanark amply justified this assertion. Kings, politicians, financiers, and reformers visited New Lanark to see the miracle for themselves. Yet in spite of this, Owen found it very difficult to convince other capitalists to undertake the same sort of experiment. Nor could he seem to interest politicians or governments in acting on his principles. For some time he was convinced that this could only be due to ignorance on their part and he made it his business to lecture and persuade all who would listen. His theme was always the same: science has now made it possible for all men to be well educated, well fed, and better behaved—if only men can be persuaded to set aside selfish interests to cooperate for the betterment of society as a whole. Over the years, however, Owen came to realize that governments and capitalists were as aware of these facts as he was, but that they had no intention of loosening their grip on society.

Deciding as had Fourier that example was the best teacher, Robert Owen now undertook to duplicate his success at New Lanark. He traveled to the United States and there organized the community of New Harmony, Indiana, in 1826, along lines which had proved successful at New Lanark. Then he returned to England to organize other communities. But Owen never seems to have realized that his success at New Lanark had been based almost entirely on his own generosity and moral strength. Three years after he had established it, the community at New Harmony dissolved in bickering, bankruptcy, and mutual recrimination. Owen's communities in England met a similar fate, and since he had sunk a large part of his fortune into their financing, he soon found himself destitute. Supported by his children, Owen devoted his remaining years to the newly established trade-union movement in England. He died in 1858, still convinced that "the happiness of self . . . [can] only be attained by conduct that must promote the happiness of the community."

It was with Saint-Simon, Fourier, and Owen that the word *socialist* first came into general use. Its first appearance in print, in fact, was as a description of Owen's principles in the *Cooperative Magazine* in London in 1826. In its most common usage it meant (and still means) any theory of social organization based on the social ownership of the means of production—factories, mines, land, and the like (as opposed, for instance, to capitalism, in which the means of production are privately owned). The word *communism,* which also came into general usage at this time, means much the same thing—the communal ownership of the means of production. Saint-Simon, Fourier, and Owen have come to be known as Utopian Socialists because, like Sir Thomas More in his *Utopia,* they supposed that human nature was such that a perfect society could come into being simply by exhortation and the application of reason to human affairs. So different is our present view of human nature that the word *utopian* has come to signify a goal impossible of achievement.

Nevertheless, the faith of the Utopian Socialists in the essential rationality of man, in his basic perfectibility, and their belief that society can be understood, controlled and organized for the welfare of all—as well as their insistence on the underlying importance of economic factors in social organization—were an important part of the intellectual climate of the world in which Karl Marx came to manhood.

But to the young student from Trier, who grew up in a Europe still recovering from the upheaval of the Napoleonic wars, torn in turn by revolutions and counterrevolutions as well as by economic depressions and the ravages of early industrialization, theoretically perfect societies seemed irrelevant. It was not enough to try to reason with men, to try to persuade them to create a new golden age. Human activity had to have deeper motives; human history, in which, after all, some progress could be traced, must be based on more scientific, more inevitable principles than mere hope, mere goodwill.

When Karl Marx arrived at the University of Berlin in the fall of 1836, he was already in search of some dynamic principle which would explain the cycles, the stages, the apparent paradoxes of human progress through history and perhaps serve as a guide to the future. He was to find it in the lectures and writing of Georg Hegel, the great German philosopher.

Hegel saw history as a process of struggle. This process he called "dialectical," in that from two opposing views a third would inevitably emerge. It is as if you are having an argument with a friend. Both of you urge your own viewpoint. But as you are arguing, a third viewpoint emerges. It combines the best of both arguments and is better than either. Thus your argument might be called a *thesis*—in that case your friend's argument would be the *antithesis*. From both arguments would emerge a *synthesis*.

Now how was this system of thought to be applied to the social and political history of man? Marx saw that society was really a way of organizing men to produce the things they needed to live by. As the technical means of production changed, so society would have to change. Social and political organization appropriate to a world in which the wheel and the lever were the only machines would hardly be appropriate to the industrial revolution. Suppose, then, we consider that feudalism —the society which existed in Europe until the seventeenth century—is the thesis. Then the needs and demands of the emerging industrial revolution would be the antithesis. From the conflict between these two— the French Revolution—comes a synthesis which is nothing other than modern capitalist society.

From his view of history Marx also arrived at the conclusion (one he shared with most philosophers of his century) that man and the world are purely material objects. There is no God, no spirit, no life after death. There is only the world which we can feel and taste and see and measure. These two views of the world—that of history as a struggle and man as a purely material being—combine to give Marxism its second name, "dialectical materialism." It was from the establishment of Marxism (dialectical materialism) as the philosophical basis for communism that a new meaning came to be attached to the word. From Marx' time on, it meant the communal ownership of the means of production, justified and explained by the philosophy of dialectical materialism. As later thinkers added their own principles to Marxism the word *communism* was modified more and more, until finally it was (as we shall see) possible to be a Marxist without being a Communist. Likewise, the word *socialist,* although often used interchangeably with the word *communist* until the turn of the century, continued to mean the social ownership of the means of production, only partially justified and explained by the philosophy of dialectical materialism and modified not at all by later Communist thinkers.

Armed with this synthesis of thought and philosophy, Marx embarked on his great work. He did not see this task as merely a study, or even a writing of history or economics. "The philosophers hitherto," he wrote, "have only interpreted the world in various ways: the thing is, however, to change it." In 1843, Karl Marx married Jenny von Westphalen, his childhood sweetheart, and took her to live in Paris. It was in Paris that he ran across the writing of a young man named Friedrich Engels. So excited was Marx by Engels' articles that he immediately entered into a correspondence with him.

Engels, two and a half years younger than Marx, had been born into a highly prosperous family of German manufacturers. Like Marx, he fell under the influence of Hegel, who was then teaching in Berlin. But Engels was a born optimist—he could never take so black a view of humanity's hopes as Marx did on many an occasion. Besides that, Engels had direct experience of the world of industry and the newly rising

41

working class. When he was twenty-one, he was sent to learn the family business in the factory city of Manchester, England. He was to manage a factory there and to fall in love with one of his workers—Mary Burns. And all his life he was to be tortured by his role as a socialist theorizer who at the same time earned his income from the sweat of the laboring classes. But he observed the condition of those classes in a way that not even Marx could. He saw how the rise of industry in Manchester had oppressed the poor so far that they now constituted a separate physical type from the rich. He saw how the factories swallowed whole families beginning with children from the age of five, how farm laborers were driven from the estates to beg in the streets of London. And above all he saw how industrialization had atomized society, making of it little more than a collection of individuals driven by greed or fear or both.

Once when he traveled into Manchester in the company of a prosperous English businessman, he remarked on the terrible misery of its working class and the widespread poverty. "And yet," the businessman replied as they parted, "there is a great deal of money made here. Good morning, sir."

The meeting of Marx and Engels, and their association over the years, was one of the great intellectual events of modern times. They complemented each other in many ways. Where Marx brought immense scholarship and dedication to his work, Engels brought a thorough knowledge of the working class and a sort of defiant exuberance. But it was always Marx who dominated the relationship. "Marx was a genius," Engels wrote years later; "the rest of us were talented at best." And where Marx tended to be extremely intolerant of those who disagreed with him and terribly impatient with followers who failed to live up to his standards, Engels never lost his sense of proportion, his humor, gaiety, and generous humility.

The two friends plunged immediately into work, theoretical and practical. The revolutionary year 1848 was near at hand; its rumblings had already been felt. Already in 1844 Marx had arrived at his idea of the working class—the proletariat as the antithesis of the capitalist system. Thus if capitalism was the thesis and the proletariat the antithesis, then from the clash of these two socialism would emerge. But in this case, since beyond the proletariat there was no other class in bondage, then socialism would represent the last historical synthesis. Beyond it lay only the gradual withering away of the state and of government as enlightened planning and leadership made such controls unnecessary in a world in which all men would receive according to their needs. In 1847, Marx and Engels wrote the *Communist Manifesto*. In brilliant compression of ideas (it only runs to fifty pages) and in emotional force it is one of the most explosive documents of all time. It makes an analysis of European society and then proposes this program of action:

(1) The forcible overthrow of the entire social order; (2) Seizure of the land by the new state; (3) A confiscatory income tax; (4) Abolition of the right of inheritance; (5) National control of banks, transport, and factories; (6) Free public education for all.

To people who used the word *justice,* Marx and Engels asked, "Justice for whom? . . . it is the proletariat who are most often caught and most severely punished." To those who spoke of liberty they pointed out that the worker could never be liberated without restricting the liberty of the employer. "Wherever the bourgeoisie [the middle-class owners of the means of production] have risen to power," they wrote, "they have left no other bond between man and man but crude self-interest and callous 'cash payment' . . . in place of many dearly bought chartered freedoms, it has set up one solitary and unscrupulous freedom—that is, freedom of trade." And with the concluding words of the *Manifesto,* Marx and Engels declared undying war on the capitalist system. "Let the ruling classes tremble at the prospect of a communist revolution. Proletarians have nothing to lose but their chains. They have a world to win. Proletarians of all lands, unite!"

When in 1848 revolutions broke out all over Europe, Marx and Engels played an active part. While rioting swept Paris and the monarchy of Louis Philippe was replaced by a republic, Marx and Engels devoted themselves to helping the small German states which were trying to throw off the shackles of Prussian militarism and social reaction. With strong connections and influence among the German labor unions, Marx quickly became a real danger to the Prussian autocrats. One day in Cologne two officers suddenly appeared at his house to kill him. Marx, dressed in his bathrobe, coolly forced them out at the point of an unloaded revolver.

However, once again, as in 1830, the 1848 revolutionary movement of the workers soon collapsed. Prussian troops occupied the petty German Rhine states; Louis Napoleon made himself emperor of the French. Marx and Engels, chased by the police of nearly every country, fled to Paris (where· Jenny Marx pawned the last of her family silver to buy food for their three children) and then, finally, to refuge in England.

While Engels worked at his double life of factory manager and revolutionary theorist, sending Marx money from time to time to keep him from starvation, Marx plunged himself into his serious work—the writing of a book on political economy which would explain history and program a campaign for socialist action. Every morning he went over to the reading room of the British Museum and every evening he wrote. He could not, in spite of poverty, find it in himself to take a steady job. Like so many of the middle-class leaders of socialism, Marx was neurotic about money. "I must follow my goal through thick and thin," he wrote, "and I shall not allow bourgeois society to turn me into a money-making machine."

What this dedication meant in human terms is graphically illustrated in a letter written by Jenny Marx after the Marxes had been evicted in 1850 for failure to pay the rent:

I shall describe to you a day in this life just as it is, and you will see that perhaps few other refugees have gone through anything like it. Since wet nurses are here much too expensive for us, I decided, in spite of continual and terrible pains in my breasts and back to nurse the child myself. But the poor little angel drank in from me so much secret sorrow and grief with the milk that he was constantly unwell. . . . He has not slept a single night since he came into the world— two or three hours at most. . . . As I was sitting like this one day our landlady suddenly appeared. We have paid her in the course of the winter over two hundred and fifty *thalers,* and we made an arrangement with her that in future we were not to pay her but the landlord, who had put in an execution. Now she denied this agreement and demanded five pounds, which we still owed her; and as we were unable to produce this sum at once, two bailiffs entered the house, took possession of all my little belongings: beds, linens, clothes, everything, even my poor baby's cradle, and the best of the toys that belonged to the little girls, who were standing by in bitter tears. . . . Our friend Schramm hurried to town to get help. He got into a cab, and the horses bolted. He jumped out and was brought bleeding into the house, where I was in misery with my poor shivering children.

The next day we had to leave the house. It was cold and rainy and dreary. My husband tried to find a place for us to live, but no one was willing to have us when we mentioned the four children. At last a friend came to our rescue, we paid, and I quickly sold all my beds in order to settle with the chemist, the baker, the butcher and the milkman, who had been alarmed by the scandal of the bailiff's arrival and who had come wildly to present their bills. The beds which I had sold were taken out of doors and loaded onto a cart—and do you know what happened then? It was long after sunset by this time, and it is illegal in England to move furniture so late. The landlord produced the police and said there might be some of his things among them, we might be escaping to a foreign country. In less than five minutes, there were two or three hundred people standing in front of our door, the whole Chelsea mob. The beds came back in. . . . [After apologizing for burdening her friend with her troubles, Jenny goes on:] The only thing that really crushes me and makes my heart bleed is that [Marx] is obliged to endure so much pettiness, that there should be so few to come to his aid, and that he who has so willingly and gladly come to the aid of so many, should find himself so helpless here.

In 1851, Marx was invited by Charles A. Dana, the publisher of *The New York Tribune,* to write a regular column. The editor of the *Tribune* at that time was Horace Greeley, who had declared himself a socialist. Marx accepted—only to turn the work over to Engels, who had a better command of English. But this income gradually declined as the *Tribune* retrenched during the depression of the fifties. In April 1855, Marx' son died at the age of eight. It was a blow from which his father barely recovered. "The house seems deserted and empty," he wrote, "since the death of the child who was its living soul . . . now I know for the first time what a genuine misfortune is. . . . I feel myself broken down."

But all during these years Marx continued steadfastly at his task. And slowly his great book *Das Kapital* grew into volume after volume.

Marx declared in *Das Kapital* that the structure of society was determined by the means with which it produced its goods—its food, clothing, machinery, and so on. Thus the means of production could be called the substructure of society. Above it, influenced by it and in turn influencing it, was a superstructure—art, religion, law, education, government, the professions. This superstructure depended in the last analysis upon the nature of the substructure. But the substructure itself was owned either by a feudal aristocracy, capitalists, or (in some of the most backward regions) slave owners. This is the basis of Marx' economic determinism—his theory of what really motivates men and institutions. Some of his followers and enemies have oversimplified this to mean that all men act only from selfish economic motives. But that was never Marx' idea. He meant only that human activities depended primarily but not exclusively on the economic organization of society.

Marx maintained that the working classes were systematically exploited by the capitalists. He reasoned that the factory worker's labor was what gave the manufactured article its value. Thus a pair of shoes, say, would be worth just the amount of labor that had gone into getting together the raw materials, shipping them to a factory, fashioning them into a pair of shoes. But with new machinery and ever-increasing efficiency, the laborer was able to produce more value of shoes in one day than he was paid wages. This difference between the worker's wages and the value of what he produced would be the capitalist's profit. Thus the capitalist steals what should be rightfully the worker's—exploits him.

Capitalism, Marx maintained, is based on deadly competition. Sooner or later small businessmen must be driven out of existence as larger and larger combines arise. As time passes, there will be fewer and fewer capitalists. At the same time the introduction of labor-saving devices will inevitably cause mass unemployment. So while capitalists grow fewer, misery increases—to the point of explosion.

Marx conceived and wrote *Das Kapital* during the worst moments in the history of the industrial revolution. From the misery and chaos around him he derived his analysis of society and its future. There were many things he did not foresee. He did not, for example, foresee that science would render irrelevant many of his objections to capitalism. Increasing technology has not, after all, brought about unemployment—just the opposite. Increasing education has made the capitalist see that his best interests have much in common with those of his workers. Wages in the most highly industrialized countries have risen tremendously. And in many industries today (automobiles are an excellent example) the workers, through their powerful unions, have almost as much control as the owners. It is, of course, only seventy-five years since Marx' theories became widely understood—too short a time to determine if all his prophecies of doom are incorrect. But the subsequent history of nations and classes seems to indicate that they are, in any case, simply irrelevant.

On the other hand, his analysis of the breakdown of

feudal society and the rise of capitalism is generally accepted as fundamentally sound. Where there remain such feudal or even slave societies in the world, a Marxist-type development has often taken place. Thus, unknown to Marx, his work was to have much more impact in such countries as Russia (where he least expected it), which were still feudal domains, than in the more advanced nations of the West.

The most serious objection to Marxism, however, remains its philosophical basis. In sweeping mysticism from human history, Marx unknowingly readmitted it in his theory of the dialectic. *Thesis, antithesis,* and *synthesis* are abstract, mystical terms with no concrete meaning. One feels that to Marx history was a real and solid being which might at any moment walk through the door of his dingy boarding house and shake his hand. Yet *history* is merely another noun. Fight as he would against it, Marx succumbed unaware to the old human vice of ascribing actuality to theory. History to him takes the place of God. It proposes and disposes, rewards and punishes; it has its own logic, to which we are helpless victims.

It is proper, however, to point out here that Marx and Engels are certainly not responsible for the twisting and misinterpretation of their theories which later took place. Marx and Engels, in spite of their total commitment to Marxist theory, never made a dogma of it. They always strove to change the theory to fit the facts. Their Communist inheritors spend most of their time changing the facts to fit the theory. Engels himself, toward the end of his life, referred to the "complete balderdash" which many Communists were making out of Marxism, while Marx once quipped that whatever else he was, he was certainly not a Marxist!

Toward the United States, Marx had conflicting reactions. During the Civil War he called the United

States government "the highest form of popular government till now realized." But later he saw it as a shield for ruthless capitalist expansion. What he never realized was that in the United States there existed no feudal background, no ancient class society. Here class was based on money—and the money kept changing hands too fast for any class distinctions to arise permanently. Thus in the United States, in spite of industrial miseries and violence, there was a chance for a truly democratic socialized society to arise. But Marx, bred and raised in an authoritarian country, immersed in the jungle of early industrialism, was never really capable of imagining democracy as we know it. What Americans have learned to take for granted he saw only as the result of chaos, war, and the dictatorship of the working classes.

A good example of the kind of event that shaped Marx' thinking was the Paris Commune of 1871. Tricked into a war with Germany, the French in 1870 suffered a disastrous defeat. Emperor Louis Napoleon was sent into exile, and a new republican government made peace with the Germans at a terrible price. The workers of Paris, feeling betrayed, refused to accept this peace. Instead they took over the government of the city in an uprising and proclaimed a Commune—a Communist-type state. With help from the Germans, the republican French government laid siege to Paris, shelling the city brutally. When the government troops entered Paris, they killed an estimated sixty thousand workers and imprisoned or exiled a hundred thousand more. Thus in a single week a capitalist republican government had destroyed more human beings than the bloody terror of the French Revolution had destroyed in three years. Was this not proof, to Marx, of the correctness of his theories? It was more than that —it was the first actual historic event in which Communist theory had actually had some effect on the course of history. "Whatever the immediate results may be," Marx wrote of the Commune, "a new point of departure of world historical importance has been gained."

As time passed, Marx' poverty was somewhat alleviated by help from Engels; but years of hard work undermined Marx' energies and health. In 1881 a pleurisy, from which he had suffered all his life, caused him to give up his work. It was in 1881 too that Jenny died of cancer. In order to visit his dying wife Marx had to leave his own sickbed to be with her. A few months later his eldest daughter died. On the fourteenth of March 1883, Engels came to call on his old friend and found the household in tears. Marx had had a hemorrhage. Going up to tell him of Engels' arrival, the maid found him slumped over his desk—asleep, she imagined. He had evidently risen from his sickbed, made his way to his desk, and sat down. When Engels entered the room, he found Marx dead.

Marx' work, carried on by Engels until his own death twelve years later, took many years to reach the public. Much to his own surprise *Das Kapital* was translated into Russian before it appeared in English. And yet, over the years, many of his books slowly seeped into the consciousness of the workers' movements in many lands. The *Communist Manifesto* has been published in almost as many languages as has the Bible. But perhaps equally as important as the monumental work of theory he left behind him was the great moral force of the example of his life. Today, in that huge segment of the world in which Marx' theories are twisted and distorted as part of the official doctrine, the figure of the man himself has the kind of moral importance for his followers that we usually reserve for saints and prophets in the West. To recognize this tremendous religious zeal, derived from the history of the rise of socialism, is the first step toward wisdom in dealing with those who inherited Marx' work.

CHAPTER TWO

1905: Dress Rehearsal

WHEN, IN THE SPRING OF 1896, Nicholas II was crowned Czar of All the Russias, there was an air of eager expectancy on the part of the Russian people. They hoped the new reign might mark the end of the dreadful tyranny of Alexander III. Nicholas' appearance, so different from that of his father, seemed to indicate a more liberal nature. He was young, well built if slender, handsome—and he sported the same kind of carefully cropped Van Dyke beard as his cousin who later became George V of England. His interests in life were of the simplest kind: hunting, fishing, riding, his family—and autocracy. For if he had learned the spartan virtues of an all-but-military education from his father, he had also been deeply indoctrinated with the divine right of kings. And from his father he had inherited an absolute state—complete with prisons, secret police, and exile areas—within which he was almost literally the father of his people, looked upon as almost divine. Russia was his private estate, and he was determined to keep it just the way he found it. But where Alexander III had been blessed with a huge frame, an iron will, a commanding appearance, and a savage cunning to maintain this position, his son Nicholas inherited none of these attributes. Rasputin once observed that the Czar "lacked insides"—and, indeed, it soon appeared that his habitual sad shyness was that of a man whose emotions had long since been frozen away into some remote corner of his being. Perhaps this was due to the violence with which his youth was surrounded. He had been present at the deathbed of his assassinated grandfather, Alexander II, and had never been allowed to forget that terrorists might strike again at any moment. For example, in 1887 a students' plot to murder Alexander III was uncovered. It came to nothing, but one of the ringleaders (who were hanged) was a student named Alexander Ulyanov. His death and his cause, which frightened Nicholas, inspired Ulyanov's younger brother Vladimir to revolutionary activity. This Vladimir Ulyanov was later to adopt the name Lenin.

Nicholas II was a dedicated diarist. Hardly a day went by on which he did not confide his thoughts to his diary. Yet over years filled with change, bloodshed, and disaster its pages record nothing more than a spiritual wilderness: "Walked long and killed two crows. Drank tea by daylight" was typical. While the revolutionary events of 1905 were shaking the empire, we find: "April 14. Took a walk in a thin shirt and took up paddling again. Had tea in the balcony. Stana dined and took a ride with us. Read." On the occasion of the dismissal of the Duma (the Russian parliament), when all the ruling classes were shaking with fright, Nicholas recorded: "July 7. Friday. Very busy morning. Half an hour late to breakfast with the officers. . . . A storm came up and it was very muggy. We walked together. Received Goremykin. Signed a decree dissolving the Duma! Dined with Olga and Petia. Read all evening."

As Trotsky observed, "An exclamation point coming after the dissolution of the Duma is the highest expression of his emotions." Count Sergei Witte, the hardheaded and able advisor of Nicholas' early years, wrote: "I wish it therefore it must be—that motto appeared in all the activities of this weak ruler, who only through weakness did all the things which characterized his reign—a wholesale shedding of more or less innocent blood, for the most part without aim." Nicholas himself, perhaps dimly aware of his shortcomings, tended to ascribe them to ill-fortune. "Whatever I try," he once wrote, "nothing succeeds. I am out of luck."

But these observations are not entirely fair. Nicholas was moved by at least one deep emotion—love for his wife, the Czarina Alix. He had married her in 1894 after a courtship lasting five years. Although the match was in part arranged by the German Kaiser Wilhelm (Alix was of German birth) and by Alix' grandmother, Queen Victoria of England, there is no doubt the young couple were deeply in love. "Wonderful, unforgettable day in my life," Nicholas confided to his diary on April 20, 1894, "the day of my engagement to my darling, adorable Alix." After their marriage Alix herself wrote into her husband's diary: "Never did I believe there could be such utter happiness in this world, such a feeling of unity between two mortal human beings. I love you—those three words have my life in them."

Alix herself was by no means weak. A convert to the Russian Orthodox Church, she displayed a superstitious fanaticism which seems almost medieval. The restrictions and obligations of royal life bored and frightened the young Czarina. She would have nothing to do with receptions, parades, public appearances. Nor did she take any pains to hide the fact that she despised the officers and aristocrats who cluttered the imperial court. This gave rise to a widespread belief that she was in fact anti-Russian. Then, to further complicate matters, by Russian law only a male child could inherit the throne. But over the years Alix gave birth only to girls—four of them. Being naturally superstitious, the Czarina sought advice of quacks and mystics. Soon the royal palace at Tsarskoe Selo outside Saint Petersburg was crawling with astrologers, spiritualists, and other fakers. And when finally Alix did give birth to a son (Alexis, born in August 1904), it appeared that he suffered from hemophilia, a condition, usually hereditary and common to European royalty, which is characterized by a tendency to profuse and uncontrollable hemorrhaging from even the slightest wounds. Doctors predicted that Alexis would not live past his eighteenth birthday. This in turn drove the Czarina to ever more desperate reliance on "holy" men —on anyone who seemed to promise some sort of cure for her child.

The young couple's reign began with a disaster. A traditional part of the coronation ceremonies in Moscow was the giving out of presents to the people on Khodinka Field. For this ceremony a huge mob had gathered. Before them, across the field, the presents (rubles, handkerchiefs, gewgaws) were displayed on stands. A whisper suddenly began to go through the crowd—there were not enough presents! The people made a frantic rush for the stands, and hundreds of women and children were trampled to death.

Another aspect of Nicholas' character soon showed itself—his deep-rooted hatred and suspicion of anyone (and there were many) more intelligent or more gifted than himself. "Nicholas was not only unstable, but treacherous," Trotsky wrote. "The Czar reserved his special caresses for just those officials whom he decided to dismiss. . . . That was a kind of revenge on the Czar's part for his own nonentity." And it was certainly true that, one after another, Nicholas' ablest ministers were dismissed until he was surrounded by men even weaker than himself. His attitude, which never changed, was perhaps best summed up in a declaration he issued when the town of Tver petitioned him for a few feeble "rights." "I shall maintain the principle of autocracy just as firmly and unflinchingly as it was preserved by my unforgettable dead father," the Czar stated.

In spite of the Czar's decrees and declarations, Russia, by the beginning of the twentieth century, was overripe for revolution. The visitor to Saint Petersburg in those years might easily have missed the deep agony of Russia's peasant and worker masses, hidden as it was behind a facade of imperial grandeur. The great palaces of the capitol, the broad boulevards, the richly dressed crowds of businessmen and aristocrats whose carriages crowded the Nevski Prospect (Saint Petersburg's Fifth Avenue), the steady booming of the midday guns in the Fortress of Peter and Paul across the river Neva from the Winter Palace—all this seemed to bespeak a permanence, an eternity of czardom. Of course beyond the Nevski Prospect sprawled vast and dreadful workers' suburbs, and the Peter and Paul fortress was crowded with political prisoners—but so things had been from time immemorial. The smoke rising from the huge new factories on the Vyborg side of the Neva, the smart crowds who attended the ballet and the opera, the hundreds of thousands of rubles which changed hands daily on the Saint Petersburg stock exchange—was this not evidence of solid prosperity?

But behind this facade lay some grim and terrible realities. The liberated serfs—about 98 percent of the population of Russia—were sinking into deeper misery. Free now from the feudal ties which had bound them to the land, they found themselves helpless victims of bankers and speculators who bought the land and then drove the peasants from it. On their own communal lands they toiled as harshly and hopelessly as ever they had on the feudal estates. By the thousand they were constantly fleeing to the already miserably over-crowded working-class quarters of the cities. But there they found themselves just as helpless and just as brutally victimized. Wages were pitifully low, prices high, hours long—an eleven-hour workday was not unusual. Unions were, of course, illegal, and all protest was savagely smashed.

Industrialization in Russia, largely financed and owned by English, French, German, and other foreign capital, came late and gave rise to a few interesting paradoxes. Thus, while Russia lagged hopelessly behind the West in such matters as railroads, communications, farm equipment, and industrial education, her factories, being new, were huge complexes. While only 17 percent of American labor worked in factories employing more than a thousand workers, nearly 50 percent of the Russian working class found themselves in such factories. This meant a heavy concentration—and the possibility of a quick mobilization of working-class strength. The fact that such a large part of Russian industry was foreign-owned, combined with widespread illiteracy, meant that those layers of management which existed between owners and workers in other countries were largely absent in Russia. Industrialization did not give rise to a large middle class in Russia; instead, the largest capitalists acted as agents of financiers and owners in other countries and exploited their own people and natural resources for foreigners. Besides that, much of Russian industry was state-owned. This meant that the government bureaucracy which managed this segment of Russian industry grew ever more powerful. Nor had the working class itself risen gradually over the ages, working out its reforms as it went. It had sprung suddenly and fresh from a traditionally revolutionary countryside. Illiterate, terribly oppressed, with no middle class to lead it, the Russian working class was open to the most advanced revolutionary ideas.

But if Russia was, to a certain extent, the victim of Western financial imperialism, she practiced an imperialism of her own at the expense of the semicivilized peoples of central and eastern Asia. Rebuffed in the Crimea from expansionist policies in the West, the czars dreamed of continental domination in the East. Taking part in the great Western "grab" on the prostrate Chinese Empire, Russia soon secured virtual dominion over Manchuria and sought to extend its powers to Korea as well. At the same time its agents never tired of playing what Kipling called their "great game" of subversion along the borders of British-held India.

Nicholas, unlike his father, seemed to have a great attraction to the idea of military conquest. He loved to dress up and play soldier. And with his deeply religious Czarina, he believed that his army was really bringing Christian civilization to the much-despised Asiatic heathens. In these expansionist dreams he was urged on by his elder cousin, Kaiser Wilhelm of Germany, who hoped to keep Russian power entangled in Asiatic adventures. But as Russian designs on Korea became more and more obvious, the Japanese grew alarmed. They had their own ambitions in this area and they felt genuinely threatened by the Russian menace. As negotiations dragged on and on, the Japanese felt they could wait no longer. Suddenly, on February 8, 1904, without a declaration of war, Admiral Heihachiro Togo's warships raided the great Russian naval base at Port Arthur, dealing the Czar's Far-Eastern fleet a mortal blow within a few hours. Japanese infantry was soon poured into Korea and Manchuria, and the Russo-Japanese War was on.

On the Russian side the war was marked by incredible inefficiency and outright scandal. The Russian commander at Port Arthur, which was considered an impregnable fortress, surrendered when he still had food and ammunition for four months. The single-track Trans-Siberian Railroad (not yet completed) proved inadequate to transfer armies to the Far East. The people and the soldiers and sailors of Russia had no interest whatsoever in this war, which was understood to be simply another of the land-grabs of the Czar. Mutiny and cowardice were everywhere.

Admiral Togo, whose place in the history of naval warfare is comparable to that of Nelson, Farragut, and Tirpitz, soon smashed up the remains of the Russian Pacific fleet and imposed a blockade of the Korean-Manchurian coast. To break this blockade, destroy the new and much smaller Japanese fleet, and gain a much-needed victory Nicholas and his war advisors determined on the simpleminded gamble of sending Russia's Baltic fleet eighteen thousand miles around the world to meet Togo in the East. Powerful but hopelessly outdated ships, staffed with green crews and fatalistic officers, were stuffed with religious icons and sent on what everybody recognized as a suicide mission in a spirit of blind gambler's folly. After a seven-month voyage marked by humiliations (the fleet almost brought on a war with England by firing on English fishing boats off the Dogger Banks in blind panic), the Russian ships reached their rendezvous with Togo in the straits of Tsushima between Korea and Japan. It took the Japanese only a day and a half to sink or capture eleven battleships, two coast-defense battleships, nine cruisers, and eleven lesser vessels. Thousands of Russian sailors perished in the most complete naval disaster in history, and even Nicholas had to admit the war was lost.

At the peace conference, which was held at Portsmouth, New Hampshire (in September 1905), under the patronage of President Theodore Roosevelt, the Russians obtained very lenient terms for their defeat. But the loss of influence in Korea and Manchuria, the explosion of the Czar's dream of conquest, were as nothing compared to the undermining of czarist authority back home. The Russo-Japanese War had created the conditions for revolution in Russia itself.

The Russian workers, whose daily life had been made even more intolerable by wartime speedups, food shortages, and prices, whose friends and brothers had perished in scandalously mismanaged battles, began a series of strikes in Saint Petersburg and Moscow at the war's end. They were led in protest by a Russian Orthodox priest named Father Georgi Gapon. Deeply religious, Father Gapon used to lecture the workers on such vices as smoking and drinking, and urge them to church while helping them organize protests for such reforms as the eight-hour day. So ineffectual had the police considered Father Gapon's revolutionary leadership in the past that they actually supported him as a sort of safety valve for the workers' anger. But in 1905 they miscalculated.

In January of that year the Saint Petersburg metal workers went on strike for four days. When this showed no effect, Father Gapon wrote a letter to the Czar: "Sire! Do not believe the Ministers. They are cheating Thee in regard to the real state of affairs. The people believe in Thee. They have made up their minds to gather at the Winter Palace tomorrow at 2 P.M. to lay their needs before Thee. . . . Do not fear anything. Stand tomorrow before the people and accept our humblest petition. I, the representative of the workingmen, and my comrades, guarantee the inviolability of Thy person. Gapon."

Nicholas' response to this letter was to leave Saint Petersburg at once with his family for the palace at Tsarskoe Selo. Behind him as a reception committee he left battalions of heavily armed police—and the inevitable troops of mounted Cossacks. The Cossacks, fierce fighters and superb horsemen, had been the last line of defense for the czars of Russia for many centuries. They were fugitive serfs originally who, during the sixteenth century, had organized into fighting bands in the region of the Ukraine. The very word *cossack* is probably derived from the Turkish *quzzak* "adventurer." Recognized by earlier czars as a potentially fine fighting force, the Cossacks had been granted all sorts of special privileges over the centuries, including local self-government. Traditionally each Cossack village was ruled by a democratically chosen council, and all Cossack land was held communally for the use of all. The Cossacks were required to enter military service at the age of eighteen and that service lasted twenty years. They provided their own horses, while the government supplied equipment. One of Alexander II's mistakes had been the granting of some of the Cossack communal land to Cossack officers and leaders for their private ownership—thereby sowing among the ordinary Cossack troops a seed of discontent which was to bear fruit in 1917. By the time of Nicholas II, there were about four million Cossacks in Russia, scattered primarily along the southern and eastern frontiers, where their military prowess made them invaluable frontier guards. Feeling themselves a very special group in Russia, pampered by the czars for centuries, the Cossacks were dependably ready to defend the crown in any confrontation with the people. And a memorable confrontation now took place.

On January 22, 1905, two hundred thousand workers and their families, led by Father Gapon, made their way in dignified procession to the Winter Palace. They carried icons and pictures of the Czar and sang "God Save the Czar" as they trudged through the icy streets. In his hand Father Gapon carried their petition—it requested an eight-hour day, a minimum wage of one ruble (fifty cents) a day, no overtime, and the calling together of a constituent assembly to draft a constitution for Russia. He had intended to hand this petition to the Czar personally while his followers waited patiently in the snow outside the palace.

The officers of the palace called upon the crowds to disperse as soon as they came into view. But two hundred thousand people cannot disband quickly. Besides, they were grimly determined to reach the Czar, who, they thought, might still grant their requests. The police and Cossacks, in panic before this immense throng, suddenly opened fire. Shooting into the dense masses of men, women, and children from a distance of about fifteen yards, they kept firing until the snow was reddened with blood. Five hundred people were killed, untold thousands wounded among the screaming, helpless crowd. On what came to be called Bloody

Sunday, Nicholas II did more than all the underground revolutionaries to give his people a lesson in what autocracy meant. Nationwide revolution was now inevitable. From Finland, where he was in hiding from the police, Father Gapon wrote to the Czar: "The innocent blood of workers, their wives and children, lies forever between thee, oh soul-destroyer, and the Russian people. . . . Let all the blood that has to be shed, hangman, fall upon thee and thy kindred!"

A veritable whirlwind of bloodshed and destruction was to follow Bloody Sunday. But it was not to be led by Father Gapon. For its leaders the Russian Revolution of 1905 turned to a new generation of revolutionaries—hardened realists who had been brought up in the awful school of czarist terror and who were dedicated to the ideas of Karl Marx.

The revolutionary movement in Russia, which had at one time centered on liberal reformist hopes (such as the Decembrist plot), had become increasingly more violent in response to the increasing violence of the czarist autocracy. The great anarchist leader Mikhail Bakunin had preached a philosophy of total destruction and had waged a losing battle with Marx for control of the international working-class movement. Marx himself, distrusting the wild and romantic formlessness of the Russian leadership, had little faith in the revolutionary prospects. "I do not trust any Russian," he wrote to Engels. "As soon as a Russian worms his way in all hell breaks loose."

Through the years of oppression a wide gap had opened between the young intellectuals of the universities in Saint Petersburg and Moscow and the peasant and worker masses. Both groups were revolutionary, but the young intelligentsia found it almost impossible to maintain meaningful connections with the illiterate masses. One group, calling themselves Narodniks, determined on a program of revolution based on the peasants. They would provide the leadership and the peasants would follow in seizing the land and then establishing a sort of utopian society based on common ownership of the land. Another group of intellectuals placed their faith in the city workers, who, with proper leadership, were to lead the rest of the country in revolt—these young men gravitated to Marxian socialism. And if these two groups disagreed on many things, they were united in one—their hatred of czarism and all it stood for.

Marxism was brought to Russia by Georgi Plekhanov, the son of a well-to-do middle-class family in the province of Tambov. Exiled from Russia for his part in terrorist activities while still a youth, Plekhanov emigrated to Switzerland. There in 1883 (the year of Karl Marx' death) Plekhanov founded the Liberation of Labor party. Formed with the help of many Russian revolutionary exiles throughout Europe, this was the first Russian Marxist party. But where Marx had foreseen revolution arising only after prolonged industrialization, where he had proposed the necessity of a middle-class revolution of the French type before a workers' socialist revolution, Plekhanov held that from the peculiarities of Russian development, "In Russia, political freedom will be gained by the working class, or it will not exist at all." Thus, instead of waiting for the weak, almost nonexistent Russian middle class to lead them through the forms of democracy, the Russian workers would have to organize and lead their own revolution.

Plekhanov also taught that the old tactics of individual terrorism were hopeless. Rather than bombs the working class needed organization—the important thing was to organize a party of agitators to lead strikes and demonstrations. Slowly but surely Plekhanov's idea seeped back into Russia. His followers were to be found in many cities. In 1898 they met secretly in the city of Minsk, where they adopted the name *Social Democrats* for their party. During this time, their rivals, the Narodniks, adopted the name *Social Revolutionaries*. Plekhanov's people soon spread a network of revolutionary activity throughout Russia. They had their own newspaper called *Iskra* (the Spark) which, though printed abroad, was smuggled into Russia in thousands of copies. They also organized the distribution of illegal literature and a means of escape for refugee leaders. By 1903 the Social Democrats were strong enough to call an international conference in Brussels. There, beyond the reach of the Russian authorities (they hoped), they would adopt an official creed and program of action. But at this moment of his greatest triumph Plekhanov was destined to lose control of his party to a young agitator from the Russian provincial town of Simbirsk. This was Vladimir Ulyanov (who had already assumed his conspiratorial name of Lenin), the younger brother of that Ulyanov executed years before by Alexander III.

Vladimir Ulyanov was born on April 22, 1870, into an upper-middle-class family in a provincial district far from Moscow and farther from Saint Petersburg. His father, a very hard-working man, rose to become Inspector of Schools for the province around Simbirsk and was entitled to be addressed "Your Excellency." His mother, of Russo-German extraction, was a devout Lutheran, and her house in Simbirsk, which was soon crowded with three sons and three daughters, looked much more like an old New England house than a Russian provincial villa. The house was a happy one, and the children did very well at school. Alexander, the eldest boy, won many medals for scholarship, and Vladimir followed suit. In 1886, Alexander went to the University at Saint Petersburg to study zoology, while Vladimir was completing his secondary education back in Simbirsk. Their father had died in that year, and Vladimir, in his elder brother's absence, was now head of the household. One day in March 1887 he was visited in his classroom by a teacher, who informed him that Alexander had been arrested in Saint Petersburg for taking part in a plot against the Czar's life. Vladimir is said to have replied, when faced by this stunning news: "That means, then, that Sasha couldn't have acted in any other way."

When his mother went to Saint Petersburg to attend her son's trial and plead for his life with the authorities there, none of the Ulyanovs' old friends or associates could be found to go with her. Soon it appeared that the family was stigmatized by Alexander's action—Vladimir learned young what guilt by association could mean. At his trial Alexander, who had taken only a minor part in the conspiracy, tried to take all the blame onto his own shoulders to protect his friends. One day in May, when Alexander's mother was still trying to win her son's life from official Saint Petersburg, she learned that he had been executed the night before. She returned to Simbirsk, where the family now lived in isolation, and carried on as if nothing had happened in order to spare the younger children. But it was already too late for Vladimir.

Alexander's cruel death hardened Vladimir. He was seventeen when he was graduated from the local academy with grades so high that the school was forced to give him the gold medal in spite of his notorious brother. But Vladimir found his further academic career blocked by the authorities, who suspected him of the same revolutionary thinking as his dead brother. Applications to universities in Saint Petersburg and Moscow were turned down abruptly. Finally Vladimir's mother got him accepted at the University of Kazan, where he started to study law. But he was seized by the police and expelled from the university when he took part in a student demonstration. It was just after this event that Vladimir first read Karl Marx. It seemed to the young student the only serious approach to the problems which beset Russia and which had brought about the death of his brother. Soon he joined a Marxist study group of other students who met secretly in the city. His mother, however, fearing for her son's life, saw to it that he was removed from Kazan to a country estate. A few weeks later the Marxist group was arrested and given heavy sentences.

Vladimir on a country estate was not a success. He once explained to his wife: "My mother wanted me to go in for farming. But I saw that it wasn't working out: my relations with the peasants became abnormal." By this he meant that any master–underling relationship was abnormal. Yet the time he spent in the country proved invaluable to Vladimir as he studied peasant problems firsthand. He also read extensively during the long nights. He started to learn German, English, French, and Italian and devoured books on political economy—sometimes with the help of a dictionary. In May 1889 his mother finally obtained permission from the authorities to allow him to take his law degree as an outside student at one of the Saint Petersburg universities. Characteristically, he learned the four-year course in less than a year and a half and then passed first in his class.

But the old stigma was still attached to the Ulyanov family. Vladimir was forced to start his practice in the far-off provincial city of Samara. Here he spent as much time studying Marx as earning a living and here he first came across the writings of Georgi Plekhanov. When the terrible famine of 1891–1892 struck the

Samara area, Vladimir was already enough of a Marxist to welcome it as a factor in stirring up peasant revolt. He refused to join in efforts to help the starving, seeing in their misery simply more pressure on the hated government. His letters to Marxists throughout Russia had, by this time, brought him to the forefront of the revolutionary movement.

In 1895, Vladimir collapsed—the doctors diagnosed pneumonia. Partly to recuperate, but mainly to get into touch with the exiled leaders of the Social Democratic party, Vladimir journeyed to Switzerland. Plekhanov was much impressed by his intellect and drive but a little disturbed by the harshness of his manner. Nevertheless, Vladimir was accepted into the movement and when he returned to Russia in October 1895, he carried seditious literature in the false bottom of his suitcase. Within three months of his return the Czar's secret police arrested him. He endured his imprisonment stoically, devoting his time to study and thought. When, after fourteen months in the cells, he was exiled to Siberia for three years, he made no protest.

Siberian exile under czarism was a uniquely Russian form of punishment. There were few guards—the prisoners traveled by themselves to their destination, and they could move within certain restricted areas as free men. They could work, get married, set up a household—the prison walls were nothing more than the frozen wastes all around them. Under these circumstances it is not surprising that Siberia became an excellent training ground for revolutionaries. There they studied, corresponded, and schemed. Lenin (Vladimir had adopted this conspiratorial name some time before) found time to continue his studies, to hunt and fish, and to think. When a young girl named Krupskaya, whom he had met a few years before in Saint Petersburg, was exiled for revolutionary activity to Lenin's district, they married and remained until the day of Lenin's death not only a devoted couple but also comrades in the revolutionary movement. For Siberian exile did little to lessen Lenin's activities. He maintained a secret but huge correspondence with the underground movement throughout Russia. His brilliant mind and his caustic wit had by now brought him into prominence and a position of leadership within the movement. When his exile came to an end in February 1900, he had already laid plans for the publication of *Iskra* and its secret distribution throughout Russia.

Reaching Switzerland again, Lenin was already recognized as the leader of the young guard of the Social Democratic movement. He joined forces with Plekhanov to edit *Iskra* and wrote a pamphlet entitled "What is to be done?" in which he proposed the idea of a small and exclusive leadership of dedicated revolutionaries rather than a broad, mass party.

The next few years were to be ones of poverty and rootless roaming for Lenin and Krupskaya. They lived in Brussels, Paris, Zurich, London—always poor, always carrying on the immense labor of organizing followers in distant Russia. When Plekhanov called for the first congress of the Social Democratic party in Brussels in 1903, Lenin was ready to challenge him for the leadership.

The question which divided this congress was whether the Social Democratic party would organize itself democratically or develop a dictatorship of the leaders of the central committee. Lenin, who was in favor of a dictatorship, threw himself into this debate with his usual vigor, and in the end his views prevailed by two votes. On this rather shaky evidence he claimed that his followers were in the majority (in Russian, *bolsheviks*), while his opponents were in the minority (in Russian, *mensheviks*). In actuality, then as later it was the Mensheviks who had a large majority within the party. Lenin's stage-managed victory at the congress soon collapsed. He lost control of *Iskra* and immediately set up a new newspaper called *Vperyed* (Forward) as a counterforce to the Mensheviks.

While the Czar was leading Russia into the shambles of defeat in the Japanese war, Lenin concentrated on his feud against the Mensheviks. But these interparty squabbles were interrupted by dramatic news from Saint Petersburg—as the Japanese war was ending in defeat, strikes and riots swept Russia.

After writing his letter of denunciation to the Czar, Father Gapon had left Finland and made his way to Switzerland, where he urged the revolutionary leaders to act quickly and decisively. But, immersed in their feuds, they paid little attention to the priest—all except a young man named Lev Bronstein, who called himself Trotsky. Trotsky was a young disciple of Plekhanov and Lenin who had gone through the same bitter school of provincial life, prison, and Siberian exile. His views, while close to theirs, were slightly different. He was more superficially brilliant than Lenin and certainly wittier. He had taken his name from that of one of his Siberian guards in the same spirit of irony which was to illuminate his writings. But a certain arrogant egotism marred his personality. Although dedicated and brilliant, he lacked a certain seriousness, a certain moral weight as compared to Lenin. Edmund Wilson has summed up this difference by pointing out that Lenin identified himself with history while Trotsky identified history with himself.

In any event, 1905 was certainly Trotsky's year to shine. He immediately made his way to Saint Petersburg and plunged into the revolutionary movement there, organizing strikes, writing pamphlets, urging means of military defense on the workers.

The terrible defeat of the Russian fleet at Tsushima had brought about a chain reaction in Russia itself. The sailors of the battleship *Potemkin* in the Black Sea mutinied and seized control of their ship. When the other ships of the fleet were ordered to fire upon her, the sailors refused to do so. And as the Czar's defeated armies straggled back to Saint Petersburg and Moscow they spread complete demoralization. Peasants rose to burn manor houses in the countryside while workers struck in the cities. Posters calling for action appeared on walls as if by magic. Into the streets poured vast and ugly crowds determined to win their rights from the autocracy. Saint Petersburg was gripped by one of the most effective general strikes in history. And now such practical matters as gunrunning and the manufacture of bombs began to assume importance. Rifles were smuggled in from America, where the revolution had much support. Mark Twain commented at the time: "If such a government cannot be overthrown otherwise than by dynamite, then thank God for dynamite."

While these events were taking place the Russian middle classes, who wished to win certain rights from the Czar but feared a complete victory of the masses, organized into a political party called the Constitutional Democrats—Cadets, for short. They demanded a parliamentary democracy along English lines, over which the Czar would rule as a constitutional monarch. They found a leader in Paul Milyukov, a well-known historian.

Thus the Czar faced three main parties of opposition: the Cadets, with their demand for democracy; the Social Democrats, with their movement toward worker-led socialism, and the Social Revolutionaries, the party of peasant socialism. To complicate matters, the Social Democrats were already split into Bolshevik and

Menshevik factions. And even for the fatalistic and autocratic Nicholas II, this opposition was too much.

Already Saint Petersburg was largely controlled by the striking workers. Under Trotsky's leadership they had set up soviets (the word means councils) of deputies in the factories and shops, which in turn sent delegates to the central Saint Petersburg Soviet. In Moscow and other cities soviets also appeared. Everywhere they disputed power with the Czar's government.

Nicholas II had no choice but to give way to this pressure. The life of his country was at a standstill, the troops unreliable, the fleet in open revolt. He issued a manifesto in which he promised Russia a constitution. Laws regarding the judicial system would also be modified, and certain land reforms were proposed. The Czar was to retain supreme control of the country, but the Duma was to have—for the first time in Russian history—certain legislative powers. These concessions, weak though they appeared, were enough to satisfy the middle-class Cadets. And when they withdrew their support from the general strike, it soon collapsed. Trotsky, as president of the Saint Petersburg Soviet, pressed for further concessions; by the device of having the workers start a run on the banks, he succeeded in winning a little more ground.

By now Lenin and Krupskaya and a few of their followers had hurried back to Russia from exile. But their arrival was too late, as was Trotsky's call for armed uprising. The people were weary of the struggle. Slowly but surely the Czar regained control of the army and navy. A new general strike, called by the Saint Petersburg Soviet, had little effect. Cossacks patrolled the streets, and Trotsky was arrested, as were other leaders. Lenin continued to lead the Moscow Soviet in rebellion for a few additional weeks—but the Army answered with artillery. Lenin and Krupskaya escaped back into exile only a few steps ahead of the police.

By New Year's Day 1906 the revolutionary movement had collapsed throughout Russia. Trotsky was given a long sentence of Siberian exile. The Revolution of 1905 had run into the sands, and the Czar's throne seemed as secure as ever.

But the defeated revolutionaries learned much from 1905. First of all, they learned that they could not count on the Cadets in a pinch. Secondly, among the revolutionaries, the Menshevik faction decided that their brief attempt to seize governmental power proved that they were not capable of ruling just yet. Much better, they said, to first set up a constitutional government by the Cadets and then educate the masses before attempting to establish socialism. The Bolsheviks learned a much more practical and important lesson; they knew now that any attempt at armed rebellion would fail unless the army was first won to support it. By themselves the masses, even with good leadership, were not capable of winning control of the government.

Nicholas II learned almost nothing from 1905. His faith in autocracy remained unshaken, and he moved quickly to take back the meager concessions he had been forced to make. Had it not been shown that revolution must fail? Had it not been demonstrated that, in the final analysis, the Cossacks and the Guards Regiments could be counted upon to drown any serious workers' uprising in blood? After 1905 the Czar and his court and the nobility and the entire vast Russian bureaucracy sank speedily back into lethargy, into their dreams of endless power, endless privilege. The masses and the Czar had met face to face, and the masses had been forced to grovel in the end. Trapped by history, the Russian ruling classes could not recognize in the events of 1905 the dress rehearsal for a much more terrible and decisive struggle ahead.

CHAPTER THREE

Prelude to Disaster

NICHOLAS, IT WILL BE remembered, under the pressure of the revolution of 1905, had promised his country a new Duma, or parliament. After countrywide elections this Duma met in Saint Petersburg in May 1906, in the Tauride Palace. The Constitutional Democrats (Cadets) had won the largest number of seats, 150. Next to them stood a party called the Trudoviks, which represented the wealthier peasants and the lower middle classes. Both these parties would be considered liberal-reformist in the West. The Duma, in the best

English tradition, opened its proceedings with an Address to the Throne. In it the politicians asked for a few reforms such as land distribution, reduction of unfair taxes, liberalization of the police grip on the nation—all of which would have been considered minimal in any Western democracy.

The Throne to which these demands were so politely addressed was now, however, once again sure of its grip on the country. Nicholas, after his fright of 1905, had determined to return to absolutism as soon as possible. He appointed a man named Ilyich Goremykin to be Prime Minister, and under him appointed a council of ministers completely subservient to the royal will. Goremykin was completely the Czar's creature, and in fact the government over which he presided, with no connections whatsoever to the Russian people or even to the middle-class Duma, represented only the Czar's personal interests.

When Nicholas II received the Duma's demand for reforms, he sent Goremykin scurrying down to the Tauride Palace to give his answer. The demands—in particular the one dealing with land reform—were simply declared "inadmissible," and that was that. When they received this answer, still in the best English tradition, the Duma liberals passed a vote of censure on the government. What they expected to accomplish by this is quite unclear. They represented only a slightly larger fraction of the Russian people than did Goremykin, but unlike him, they had no control whatsoever over the armed forces. Since the revolutionary parties —the Bolsheviks, Mensheviks, and Social Revolutionaries—had completely boycotted the elections, the Duma did not even have the means of calling out the street mobs. In any event, it is very unlikely that these would have answered any summons. They had suffered too cruelly just the year before.

The Duma therefore did the only thing it could do. It made angry speeches. It made angry speeches for two months. Then, on July 22, 1906, when the Duma deputies arrived at the Tauride Palace, no doubt to make more angry speeches, they found it surrounded by the Czar's troops, the doors bolted and barred against them. The Duma, they were informed, had been dissolved by the Czar.

When some of the deputies appealed to the people for support, they met only indifference. And this was the pattern that parliamentary government, or that limited form of it permitted by Nicholas II, was to take in the remaining years of his rule. There was still no such thing as personal freedom, freedom of speech, freedom of the press. The peasants continued to labor under heavy exploitation, the demands of the workers continued to be ignored. From time to time, driven by necessity, the Czar would call the Duma together in an attempt to round up popular support. But each time he found that even these very conservative representatives of the rich could not stomach his policies—and the Duma would again be dismissed amid many reproaches and futile protests.

In the spring of 1906, Nicholas replaced Goremykin as Prime Minister with Peter Stolypin. Stolypin had several virtues to recommend him for the job. First of all, he had a cynical attitude toward the Duma, seeing it as a means of controlling the people rather than representing them. Second, he had dealt ruthlessly with the revolutionaries of 1905 as the Czar's governor in the province of Saratov. Third, he managed to convince the Czar that his program of land reform might steal the thunder from the revolutionary movement.

Stolypin was personally very capable, courageous, intelligent, and determined. He knew exactly where the Czar's best interests really lay and tried mightily to gain them. He inaugurated a program of selling state-owned land to individual peasants and making it easier for them to buy privately owned land. This, he reasoned with justification, would soon produce a class of peasant owners as immune to revolutionary appeals as the French peasant-owner class had been ever since the French Revolution. Besides that, he opposed the Czar's wish to abolish the Duma. Let us simply manage the Duma, much as we manage the other governmental departments, he advised. He also tried hard to inject some vigor, some efficiency into the government itself.

Stolypin's plans bore fruit. So far as the peasants were concerned, Lenin was forced to admit: "If this [program of land reform] should continue for a long period of time . . . it might force us to renounce any agrarian program at all. It would be empty and stupid democratic phrasemongering to say that the success of such a policy in Russia is impossible. It is possible!" And, of course, without peasant support no revolutionary movement could succeed in Russia. But if the revolutionaries feared Stolypin, it soon developed that the ruling classes feared him even more.

Never able to tolerate a man of ability for very long, Nicholas grew to distrust and secretly hate his Prime Minister. In this he was supported and egged on by the Czarina Alix, who detested Stolypin because he opposed the promotion of her favorite friends. And of course the Duma, which Stolypin treated with open contempt, cordially returned his feelings. In any event, the problem was resolved for all concerned on September 14, 1911. On that evening Stolypin attended with the Czar (though seated separately) an opera in Kiev. During the second-act intermission pistol shots rang out. Stolypin rose with a stunned look on his face and blood on his uniform. He made the sign of the cross and then died. The Czar appears to have been genuinely horrified by the event, even though he probably welcomed it. The assassin, a young man named Dmitri Bogrov, was caught on the spot and whisked away by the police for secret questioning and speedy execution. It was given out that he was a "terrorist"—but long afterward it appeared that he may well have been a police agent.

If it seems horrifyingly incredible that a police agent should murder the Prime Minister or that such an accusation should be at least reasonable, it would be well to remember that all during the years of czarist autocracy a huge and self-sufficient police and secret-police empire had been built up in Russia. The people hated and loathed these police, called the "Pharaohs." They were everywhere—a well-armed, well-disciplined private army responsible only to the Czar, but so vast that even the Czar knew little of all their activities. Secret police agents spied on everyone—from revolutionaries to the highest members of the nobility and government. They even spied on members of the Czar's family. Their meticulous and well-reasoned reports accumulated over the years in mountains of evidence so huge that it later took a decade to sort it all out. Besides spies, the Russian secret police specialized in *agents-provacateur*. These were men who were insinuated into organizations—into all the revolutionary parties, into the Duma, into intimate circles of the nobility—who made a practice not only of spying and betraying but also of urging ill-considered and dangerous action. In this way they often forced people to commit actions for which they could easily be arrested or which would lead to disaster.

The czarist police included men of hardheaded realism. Their reports give a much clearer evaluation of events than do the reports of the Czar's ministers. But their empire of brutality, murder, espionage, and betrayal had earned them the hatred of the masses. They, better than anyone, knew they could expect no mercy whatsoever from a revolution, so all their energies were bent on a desperately realistic attempt to forestall such an uprising. It was in this spirit that they spied on the most powerful man in Russia, the man who gained a unique and commanding influence over the Czarina and, through her, the Czar: Gregory Rasputin.

Rasputin, born in 1871 in the far-off Tobolsk province of Siberia, was, like his father before him, essentially a rowdy peasant. He soon developed a reputation in his home town as a horse thief, drunkard, seducer of young girls, and general good-for-nothing. He had no education and remained largely illiterate all his life. His one apparent attribute was great physical strength. He was a coarse-featured man with a heavy black beard and strangely piercing eyes.

When he was thirty, Rasputin abandoned his wife and three children (much later on a visit home he beat up his aged father in the town square) and, claiming that he had seen the light of God, took to the road as a holy beggar. He preached, to anyone unwise enough to listen, the age-old doctrine that one must sin before one could expect forgiveness. One must sin especially if one were an attractive woman. And as Gregory was holy enough to stand any amount of sinning, one could do worse than to sin with him. Simpleminded? Yes, but the dark night of oppression calls forth such eccentric philosophies—the Dark Ages in Europe (which in some respects still prevailed in Russia) saw the rise of many such sects. Russia, in which peasants of some drive or intelligence were smothered by lack of education and opportunity, was full of such so-called holy men at the time. They were only symptomatic of the decay of society.

But Rasputin was slightly different. He was, without doubt, an extremely intelligent schemer, an excellent judge of character, and more than that—he seems to have been something of a hypnotist. In any event he soon made his way to Saint Petersburg, was adopted into some of the circles of the nobility, and eventually found himself presented to the Czar and Czarina. Nicholas' arid diary records in November 1905: "We got acquainted with a man of God, Gregory, from Tobolsk Province." And Rasputin soon established himself as the favorite of both Czar and Czarina. Favorite is perhaps too weak a word. He was a mentor to the family, a guide, a father-confessor, and, most dangerous of all, an advisor in whom they had blind faith. Ministers were appointed or dismissed at Rasputin's wish, state policy decided by his whim. He soon became the uncrowned real ruler of Russia.

During this time Rasputin never changed his personal habits. The police spies who faithfully dogged his tracks sent in reports of fantastic behavior by this holy man. "He returned today at five o'clock in the morning completely drunk." "On the night of the 25th–26th the actress V. spent the night with Rasputin." "He arrived with Princess D. (the wife of a prominent noble) at the Hotel Astoria." "Came home from Tsarskoe Selo about eleven o'clock in the evening." "Rasputin came home with Princess Sh— very drunk. . . ." As Trotsky acidly observed: "Thus for months and years the melody was played on three keys: 'Pretty drunk,' 'Very drunk,' and 'Completely drunk.'" And Prince Felix Yussupov, hardly a revolutionary, wrote of him: "His life in Saint Petersburg became a continual revel, the drunken debauch of a galley slave who had come into an unexpected fortune." Mikhail Rodzianko, the portly president of the Duma, reported: "I had a whole mass of letters from mothers whose daughters had been dishonored by this insolent rake."

Yet these reports had no effect on the Czar or Czarina. They referred to Rasputin as The Friend in their correspondence. "During vespers I thought so much about our Friend," the Czarina once wrote to the Czar, "how the Scribes and Pharisees are persecuting Christ pretending that they are so perfect . . . yes, in truth no man is a prophet in his own country." To police reports of Rasputin's carousals she wrote: "They accuse Rasputin of kissing women, etc. Read the apostles; they kissed everybody as a form of greeting."

Rasputin used his power thoroughly and whimsically. Thus, when one of the police spies asked him why he was so thoughtful during one of his drunken orgies, the holy man replied that he could not decide whether or not to convene the Duma. And the Czarina's notes to the Czar are full of such advice as "Our Friend says that Stürmer may remain a few days longer as President of the Council of Ministers." Anyone of whatever rank or influence who hoped to reach the Czar had first to pay his respects to Rasputin.

What did Rasputin represent in a deeper analysis? His career has something about it of the carefree savagery of Caligula, who, in one theory, behaved as he did simply to underline and rub the noses of the Roman aristocrats into the terrible fact of arbitrary power. It was as if Rasputin were shouting: "Very well, we live in a completely decadent, savagely repressive, absolutely pointless society. Now I will force you by my wild excesses to recognize the filth around you!" There is, of course, no evidence to prove that this was his consciously held view. Yet it is inadmissible to assume that any man is simply all black, all devil. But with Rasputin we come very close to that.

Rasputin's influence with the Czarina was based mainly on her continuing fear, which developed into morbid dread, for her son's life. Rasputin seemed able to stop the young boy's internal bleeding when he was injured simply by staring at him. There is now scientific evidence to show that hynotism can accomplish this. The Czarina thought Rasputin's powers stemmed from holiness.

As the years went by Rasputin's hold over the royal family grew greater and greater. Unknown to Nicholas or his wife, there was a deeper social reason for this. In the gathering storm of social disaster the Russian ruling class, like such classes before in history, finding that they had no connections or roots or support from any segment of society, turned to the miraculous to save them from impending doom. Their situation was so precarious that subconsciously they recognized the need of divine intervention to save them. "If there had been no Rasputin," a czarist senator later remarked, "it would have been necessary to invent one." It may have been this very need which caused the aristocracy to hate Rasputin more venomously.

After Stolypin's assassination Nicholas appointed one of his own inept flatterers Prime Minister. Thus Count Vladimir Kokovtsov came to power in 1911. It was during his administration that revolutionary activity, which had reached a standstill in the preceding years, again grew throughout Russia. The number of people taking part in political strikes increased dramatically from 1909 to 1912. And in October of that year striking miners at the Lena gold fields were shot down by police in a smaller repetition of the Bloody Sunday massacre. Things slid from bad to worse. Count Kokovtsov lost favor with the Czarina because of his antipathy to Rasputin and was finally replaced by the old czarist war horse Goremykin, who, though now seventy-four and ill, took up once again the post of Prime Minister in the early months of 1914. Nothing had changed, it seemed. Nicholas presided over the misery of nearly two hundred million people with complete satisfaction that he would rule so till the end of his days.

Meanwhile the revolutionaries, shattered by their defeat in 1905, painfully and slowly rebuilt their organizations. Trotsky, the hero of 1905, had been condemned to exile in Siberia. But he soon found means of escaping by hiding under a wagon of hay. He made his way across Europe to Switzerland, where he found Lenin and the other exiles engaged in their endless feuds as to who would control the Social Democratic party and whose policies would prevail. Over the years there were several conferences. Confused and confusing arguments—attacks, retreats, compromises—made an endless round within the movement. But in general the Menshevik faction, led by Plekhanov and his younger associates, Irakli Tseretelli, Julius Martov, and Fyodor Dan, continually sought to make the Social Democratic party a legal, broadly based and governed organization which would use legal means to achieve power. They were utterly opposed to terrorism and violence. Lenin, on the other hand, helped by such new associates as Maxim Litvinov, Lev Kamenev, and Grigori Zinoviev in leading the Bolshevik faction, maintained that it was ridiculous to expect to take over the government without a violent struggle. And since the masses remained illiterate and poorly organized, it would still be necessary to lead them by means of a tightly organized, dictatorial secret committee.

A much more important difference grew between Mensheviks and Bolsheviks during these years. The Mensheviks felt that it would be necessary at first to cooperate with such middle-of-the-road parties as the

Cadets in order to set up a democratic government. Only the middle classes, they thought, would be capable of managing the intricate machinery of government. If this meant inevitably a long period of capitalist development in Russia and a postponement of the socialist revolution, they were willing to wait. Lenin, on the other hand, although he appeared sometimes to waver, maintained that no compromise or arrangement was possible with the Russian middle classes or their party. They were too weak, too frightened of the masses, he argued. And why, he demanded, should the masses of the Russian people endure a capitalist period of exploitation when they could seize the power (which he was certain they would quickly learn to manage) and plunge directly into socialism?

The argument and its variations raged for years. Sometimes Lenin appeared to be winning, at other times the Mensheviks had control. A particular bone of contention was which faction was to control the new Social Democrat newspaper *Pravda* (Truth). The management passed from one group to the other but finally wound up in the hands of the Bolsheviks. The newspaper, with a circulation (illegal, of course) of forty thousand in Russia, became a potent weapon in Lenin's hands. But over the years it appeared that the Mensheviks, in spite of their name, retained a large majority within the Social Democratic movement.

Another aspect of these years of exile was the way in which the revolutionaries secured funds to carry on. This they accomplished by relying on the activities of small bands of highly trained and dedicated men who would rob banks, post offices, and other institutions in Russia and send the money abroad for revolutionary work. In one such operation, in Tiflis, the raiders made off with 324,000 rubles ($162,000). It was in this raid that a young man named Josef Djugashvili, a Bolshevik, distinguished himself. Although he worked hard for the party, he was as yet too young to enter into its inner circle. When he finally did, years later, he had already adopted his conspiratorial name—Stalin.

The life of political exile was a hard and wearing one. Besides the endless arguments, the endless scurrying for money, there were many personal privations and exasperations to which exiles were subjected. For one thing there were the numerous police spies sent out from Russia to infiltrate, betray, and disrupt the movement. More than one of these men reached a high position in the party before being exposed. Their presence made for a general and widespread feeling of suspicion and dread. Then, too, cut off from their roots in Russia for years on end, the exiles developed the depression and hysteria of those who have no home. Many committed suicide, others sold out to the police, some simply drifted into drunken oblivion. The subjugation of the workers in Russia after 1905, the land reforms of Stolypin, the seemingly endless power of the Czar gradually wore down revolutionary morale. On more than one occasion Lenin himself confided to friends that he did not expect to live to see the revolution. But Lenin never permitted himself to be demoralized. His life was kept full and busy by writing and study. And in his wife Krupskaya he had a firm support. As he submerged himself more and more into the historical drama of his times he, like Marx, began to assume an almost mythical stature in the eyes of his followers. His uncompromising attitudes, his harshly argumentative ways were overcome by his supreme ability to cut to the core of any problem and explain it in simple words. Men who came to him in confusion, or even with hostility, soon found themselves gripped by a logic so complete, realistic, and persuasive that they became his disciples. Thus during the years his following grew. It has been estimated that there were thirty thousand Bolsheviks in Russia by 1914. And if the Mensheviks continued to maintain a majority of the revolutionary movement, nevertheless Lenin's minority were more dedicated, more ruthlessly committed to the struggle. But all the frustrations, arguments, plots, and schemes were soon to be overshadowed by the sudden plunge of Europe into general disaster.

Nicholas' foreign policy, which had bruised the autocracy in the Japanese war, remained vaguely expansionist. But as Russia was in no condition to undertake foreign conquests, this expansionism found a different outlet. This was the policy of Pan-Slavism. Half-mystical, half-clever, Pan-Slavism proclaimed Russia the protector of all Slavs everywhere. The vague ties of blood and language were supposed to bind the Slavs together in much the same way as Hitler's conception of race was later supposedly to bind Germans together. But the Slavs, viewing themselves realistically at that time, did not claim to be supermen.

In any case Russia was the self-proclaimed protector of the Slav nations of the Balkans such as Bulgaria, Serbia, and Bosnia. This policy ran head-on into the ambitions of the creaking Austro-Hungarian Empire in that area. Small but savage wars, inflammatory nationalism, subversion, and plotting kept the Balkan pot boiling until, in the summer of 1914, a Serbian-backed terrorist organization assassinated Austrian Archduke Franz Ferdinand in the streets of Sarajevo. Immediately Europe realized that it was about to slide into war. The Austrians presented a harsh ultimatum to Serbia. When it was accepted, they nevertheless declared war on their tiny neighbor. Since it would be unthinkable for Russia to stand aside while a Slav nation was conquered, Nicholas ordered a general mobilization. But Austria's great ally Germany could not permit the tottering Hapsburg empire to be defeated. They demanded an end to Russian mobilization. While distraught foreign ministers frantically sought some means of escape from the impending calamity, the Russians refused the German ultimatum and, on August 1, 1914, Germany declared war on Russia.

Since late in the nineteenth century Russia had maintained a treaty of alliance with France. As the two nations who felt most menaced by Germany's rise to power, the absolutist government of the Czar and the republican government of France had planned a carefully calculated response to any German aggression. That this alliance between a republic and the czardom was unnatural was something that worried the Russian ruling classes as much as it bothered the French socialists. But necessity forced the pact. And so, when Germany mobilized against Russia, France mobilized against Germany. French persuasion, combined with the German advance into neutral Belgium, dragged Great Britain into the struggle on the Franco-Russian side. Thus the precarious balance of European peace tumbled down like a house of cards, and the armies marched.

The war, which came as a stunning surprise to the masses of the Russian people, at first enlisted their enthusiastic support. The mounting waves of strikes and protests which had been plaguing the government suddenly vanished, to be replaced by huge demonstrations in favor of the Czar. Earlier hatreds were drowned in one overwhelming hatred of Germany. Mobs spontaneously burned the German Embassy in Saint Petersburg. Huge crowds filled the churches to dedicate themselves to victory. A vast multitude heard the Czar swear he would not make peace until Germany was defeated and then knelt and sang "God Save the Czar" with devout fervor. The name of the capital was changed from the German-sounding Saint Petersburg to the more Russian Petrograd. Patriotic decrees were greeted enthusiastically by the people, who went so far as to submit to the new law banning the sale of vodka to prevent drunkenness. That the sale of vodka was a government monopoly and that by discontinuing it the government was itself cutting off one of its major sources of income occurred to no one. The neglected and mistreated Duma roused itself to vote almost unanimously to support the war. The regiments marched off to the front cheering the Czar. Somehow, in some magical way, all Russia's problems were to be solved by the coming bloodbath. Furthermore, no one doubted that Germany would be quickly defeated.

At first everything seemed to go well. The French and Russians were well aware that Germany would strike first at France. In order to save France from instant defeat it was necessary that Russia begin an immediate offensive against Germany in the east, thereby draining German divisions from the critical onslaught in the west. And on paper this seemed logical. The Russian army had undergone some reforms since the disaster of 1905. Munitions factories had been built, railroads extended, training revised. And, in any event, the huge masses of Russian manpower (her army was to total fifteen million men) were expected to tell heavily against the Germans. The Russian "steamroller" might be creaky and slow to start, but once it was in motion, it was expected to flatten all opposition. Thus, two weeks after mobilization, two Russian armies were flung against the thin German lines in East Prussia.

But behind the facade of Russian power existed a vacuum of leadership and supplies. The overall command of the armies was entrusted to the Czar's second cousin, Grand Duke Nicholas, a man who understood little of modern war. The ancient and often corrupt generals under him proved utterly incompetent. At the head of the war ministry stood the figure of General Vladimir Sukhomlinov, a man who boasted that he had not read a military manual for twenty-five years and who placed his faith in bayonet warfare and cavalry charges. He was openly accused of selling information to the Germans, and though these charges were unfounded, they reflected the great lack of confidence felt everywhere in the high command. It is hard to imagine how ill-equipped for modern warfare the Czar's huge army was. Thousands had no shoes, one man in three had no rifle, artillery was in pitifully short supply, munitions even shorter. In such matters as wireless, airplanes, transportation, the Russian Army proved helpless. The lack of wire for field telephones and the lack of code books on most command levels impelled the two Russian armies advancing on East Prussia to communicate with each other in clear on the radio. Picking up their messages, the German commanders Erich Ludendorff and Paul von Hindenburg were able to prepare the great catastrophe of Tannenberg in which both Russian armies were annihilated. But if hundreds of thousands of peasants perished in this calamity, the Russian offensive did at least serve its purpose in drawing German strength from the Western Front. The Battle of the Marne was, in a sense, won in the forests of East Prussia.

Only against the Austro-Hungarian Empire did Russian troops do well. There, faced by an army as graft-ridden, poorly led, and ill-equipped as their own, the Russians won overwhelming victories. But all of these came to nought when, after the Western Front stabilized into its grim trench warfare, the Germans threw their weight to the east. Then a great retreat commenced. Divisions, armies, thousands and soon millions of men were fed into the holocaust by the desperate Russian commanders. But defeat followed defeat, and vast areas of Russia fell under German domination. As part of their retreat the Russian commanders laid waste the countryside behind them and drove the population eastward. This had the effect of pouring huge masses of discontented refugees into the back areas.

The only limit to the German advance was that imposed by their own caution. The war minister, General Vladimir Sukhomlinov, was disgraced and replaced by one Polivanov, who replied to questions regarding the front by stating, "I place my trust in the impenetrable spaces, impassable mud, and the mercy of Saint Nicholas Mirlikisky, Protector of Holy Russia." General Nikolai Ruszky, commander of the Northern Front, confessed: "The present-day demands of military technique are beyond us. At any rate we can't keep up with the Germans." Attempts by England and France to supply Russia with technicians and supplies were completely inadequate, and when they tried to reach Russia through the Dardanelles, they suffered a bloody defeat.

As months of disaster followed each other the liberal members of the Duma, the nobility, and the General Staff increasingly blamed defeat upon the czarist bureaucracy. It was rumored that the Czarina was in secret league with the Germans. Rasputin's evil influence grew to be more and more hated. The ruling classes feared (correctly) that the masses would not stand the war much longer. Some advocated a separate peace with Germany as the only way of preventing a revolution, while others talked and plotted about removing the Czar and substituting some other figure on the throne. But always these aristocratic plots for a change in the government ran up against the cold fear that any tampering with the czardom would ignite a popular mass revolution that would sweep everything away before it. But the plotters nonetheless did manage to get rid of Rasputin. Years before, Rasputin had predicted that the Romanov dynasty would not survive his own death. But with the coming of the war, death was very far from Rasputin's mind. His influence in the royal establishment grew as hysteria rose over Russian defeats. When, in 1916, against the advice of his councilors, Nicholas assumed command of the armies and departed for the front, Rasputin and the Czarina were left behind to rule Russia as they willed. Ministers were dismissed, laws passed, decrees promulgated. Very soon practically all the high government positions were filled by Rasputin's creatures. The Duma fumed and argued about it but did nothing. Protests were dealt with harshly, and the Czarina kept Nicholas constantly informed and inflamed about events. "I am firm, but listen to me—this means our Friend, and trust us in everything." To the mounting waves of criticism the Czarina replied by urging the Czar: "This must be your war and your peace . . . and not by any means the Duma's. They have not the right to say a single word in these matters." And again and again: "Bring your fist down on the table. Don't yield. Be the boss. Obey your firm little wife and our Friend." On December 13, 1916, she writes: ". . . people want to feel your hand . . . 'Russia loves to feel the whip.' That is their nature."

But the Russian nature did not, after all, differ very greatly from that of any other people. The misled, unequipped, and thoroughly demoralized army was already beginning to disintegrate. Soldiers deserted by the thousands, regiments refused orders, officers were murdered as the slaughter continued. And the usual punishments—flogging and the firing squad—could not stem the tide. The soldiers began to listen now to those among them who were revolutionaries. The influence of Mensheviks, Bolsheviks, and Social Revolutionaries grew daily, while the continued liberal support for the war lost the Duma parties the confidence of the troops. Having lost untold millions of comrades and endured an unimaginable nightmare of fighting and defeat, the Russian soldier desperately wanted peace—at any price. He had long since lost confidence in victory, then in his leadership, and now in the government. But who were these soldiers? They were, of course, the peasant masses of Russia. So, as millions upon millions of men were called to the colors and underwent the savage lessons of the war, the bulk of the Russian population was learning some very costly and extremely useful political lessons.

And while their homeland sank into defeat and chaos, what of the exiles—Lenin, Trotsky, Plekhanov, Martov, Dan, and the others? Some of them, along with their German and French and British colleagues, immediately became ardent patriots as soon as war was declared. In spite of all their resolutions about the unity of the working class, these socialists voted large sums of money for the war effort and gave their support to their individual nations as savagely as the most conservative General Staff could have wished. The impact of this betrayal of their ideas upon Lenin and some of his followers was tremendous. At first he refused to believe it. But as he realized that socialists throughout Europe were jumping onto the bandwagon of patriotism, his determination only hardened. Living in Switzerland with Krupskaya, he gathered around him those socialists who opposed the war. In the spring of 1916 he published a small book entitled *Imperialism: The Last Stage of Capitalism* in which he sought to bring Marx up to date by analyzing the contradictions and entanglements which had plunged capitalist Europe into catastrophe. Above all he hammered hard on the theme of converting what he called the imperialist war into civil war in the various countries. Making good use of the Marxist means of analysis, he never tired of exposing the war as a conflict of international capital in which the workers were simply cannon fodder. By sticking resolutely to his principles, through his writings and through the moral force of his personality, Lenin was now the undisputed leader of the Bolsheviks scattered throughout Russia. The anti-Boshevik historian Nikolai Sukhanov declared: "The whole Bolshevik effort was kept inside the iron frame of the spiritual center abroad, without which the party workers felt themselves completely helpless, in whose presence they were proud to stand, and to which the best of them regarded themselves as devoted and dedicated servants, like Knights of the Holy Grail."

But, however holy they may have felt themselves, Bolsheviks, like their rivals the Mensheviks and Social Revolutionaries, thought themselves powerless before the whirlwind of war and disaster which had overtaken their country. With mass discontent beginning to replace patriotic fervor throughout Russia, they still did not feel confident enough to call for an uprising. Although it could be only a question of time before rebellion broke out, it was to be sparked, not by the revolutionary leadership, but by the nobility.

Foreseeing the impending disaster, and living in real fear and trembling at the approaching social revolution, a small group of nobles and liberals determined to do away with Rasputin and thus bring the Czar back under some sort of reasonable control. Their scheme, which Trotsky characterized as "a moving-picture scenario designed for people of bad taste," was nevertheless carefully worked out. The moving force behind the plot was Prince Felix Yussupov. It was he who invited Rasputin to supper in his house on December 29, 1916. There he stuffed the huge holy man with poisoned cakes and poisoned drink. The potassium cyanide seemed to have no effect upon him. Yussupov grew frightened, and his coconspirators who waited upstairs grew nervous. Was it just barely possible that this madman's claims were true? How much poison could any man swallow and remain standing?

To keep up their spirits the group played an old record of "Yankee Doodle" over and over again on the phonograph. Finally Yussupov could stand no more. When Rasputin demanded and swallowed still another glass of poisoned wine, Yussupov produced a pistol and shot him. Rasputin crashed to the floor with a shout, and the other conspirators hurried down the stairs. Finding Rasputin apparently dead, they all retired back upstairs to consider their next move.

After a brief discussion Yussupov went again to look at the dead man. Rasputin's eyes twitched open, and to Yussupov's hysterical horror he gripped his shoulder and, when the prince fled back upstairs, clambered up behind him on all fours, bursting with a roar into the midst of the conspirators. In the ensuing panic two shots found their way to Rasputin's heart, and he at last fell dead while the conspirators went out of their minds with hysteria. His body—still warm, it was said—was finally bundled into the automobile of the Grand Duke Dmitri and hurried to the river Neva, where it was pushed beneath the ice. The next day, all Petrograd had heard the news. While the grief-stricken Czarina knelt by Rasputin's grave (his body had been recovered from the Neva on January 1, 1917) and the Czar hurried home from the front to console her, practically all the citizens, high or low, of Petrograd showered congratulations and thanks upon the murderers.

Now, at last, it seemed as if some sort of rational order might replace the governmental chaos. It was as if some dreadful nightmare had ended. But these feelings were confined to the ruling classes. Rasputin's death, which appeared to clear the way for some sort of liberal reform, left the misery of the vast mass of the Russian people unchanged. The millions of dead, the demoralized army, the hundreds of thousands of deserters, the toiling factory workers who could no longer afford even the barest necessities of life, the mutely suffering peasants—for them the death of Rasputin had only one effect. It proved beyond any shadow of doubt that the government was so corrupt that even its supporters, even a grand duke or a prince, had no other means of affecting it than through murder. The medieval orgy of absolutism had reached its highest expression in the disgusting rise and fall of Gregory Rasputin. Now the masses would have their say.

CHAPTER FOUR

The February Revolution

NONE OF THE LEADERS expected it. Neither the Bolsheviks nor the Mensheviks nor the Social Revolutionaries nor the liberals nor the czarist nobility. Even though they had prayed for it or feared it or predicted it in a general way, when it occurred, none of them was prepared. The only organization in Russia that accurately forecast what was about to happen was the secret police. But their perceptions were keener—just as the perceptions of a man facing the charge of a ferocious tiger are keener than those of his gun-bearers far behind him. The February Revolution (which in our calendar took place in March 1917) that exploded in the streets of Petrograd caught not only its leaders and opponents unaware—in a certain sense it caught the people themselves unaware. It was something that grew on unexpected success—an event fed by its own flames, a movement which surprised itself by its own victory.

A revolution, when it occurs, offers the greatest challenge to any historian. The masses of people fighting and dying in the streets do not take time out to keep a journal of what they are doing. In any case their victories and defeats are often isolated one from another. A man immersed in a struggle has no time to raise his head to take an overall look at events. After the fact there will be memoirs—but those who write them will often have some special axe to grind. And, too, one of the first objectives of the mob will be to burn and destroy the records. When to this is added the fact that the vast majority of the people who took to the streets in Petrograd were barely literate, it will be seen how difficult is the historian's task. And yet it is possible to reconstruct the intensely dramatic events which brought about the downfall of the Czar during five days of struggle—by imagination, careful selection of the records which do exist, and above all by sticking firmly to the inner social meaning of these events.

It has been said that the February Revolution was leaderless. It is true that the various party organizations were caught unprepared and that the higher leaders of the parties were in exile or prison at the time. But over the years, in Russia, a very highly politically educated leadership had been developed among the workers themselves. Bolsheviks, Mensheviks, Social Revolutionaries of the lower ranks were accustomed to explaining things to their fellow workers in the factories, their fellow soldiers in the ranks. They were used to organizing, to leading. If they lacked the grip on theory and philosophy displayed by such as Lenin, Plekhanov, Trotsky, they nevertheless understood immediate political problems and how to exploit them. Besides that, they had all been schooled in the ruthlessness of the czarist state; many had had experience of street fighting in 1905.

Before unfolding the drama of the revolution, it might be well to see what sort of people these lower-rank revolutionaries were. Remember that they were of every political persuasion, not just Bolshevik, so long as it was revolutionary. Max Eastman, who visited Russia in the 1920's, has sketched the following portrait of them: "A wonderful generation of men and women was born to fulfill this revolution in Russia. You may be traveling in any remote part of the country, and you will see some quiet, strong, exquisite face in your omnibus or your railroad car—a middle-aged man with white, philosophic forehead and soft brown beard, or an elderly woman with sharply arching eyebrows and a stern motherliness about her mouth, or perhaps a middle-aged man, or a younger woman who is still sensuously beautiful, but carries herself as though she had walked up to a cannon—you will inquire, and you will find that they are the 'old party workers.' Reared in the tradition of the terrorist movement, a stern and sublime heritage of martyr-faith, taught in infancy to love mankind, and to think without sentimentality, and to be masters of themselves, and to admit death into their company, they learned in youth a new thing—to think practically; and they were tempered in the fires of jail and exile. They became almost a noble order, a selected stock of men and women who could be relied upon to be heroic, like a Knight of the Round Table or the Samurai, but with the patents of their nobility in the future, not the past."

Rasputin's body had been recovered from the Neva on New Year's Day. Aside from general rejoicing at his death, there was no immediate reaction. The murderers, too close to the royal family to be hanged, were banished to their country estates. The Czarina spent her days praying beside Rasputin's tomb, while the Czar tried to comfort her. The Duma continued its endless bickerings, the generals continued their endless mistakes, and the severe winter mantled Petrograd in snow and ice.

Food supplies, which had been a gold mine of graft to the ruling classes, were in shorter supply than ever. On March 1, 1917, bread rationing was introduced in Petrograd. Now long lines of women could be seen, sometimes waiting through the icy night for a chance to purchase a few ounces of bread. The misery of the people, now reaching its height, had no effect on the Czar. When the English and French ambassadors, alarmed by the situation, begged him to take some action to regain his people's confidence, Nicholas replied: "Do you mean that *I* am to regain the confidence of my people, Ambassador, or that they are to regain *my* confidence?"

Strikes took place in some of the factories in response to rationing, but nothing spectacular. The Duma which met on February twenty-seventh called angrily for an end to the war and for the usual reforms —sounds that had been heard before. The president of the Duma, Mikhail Rodzianko, wrote a note to Nicholas warning that revolution was imminent—but the frightened cries of the liberals had also been heard before. On March eighth Nicholas once again left the capital to resume his duties at the front, hundreds of miles to the south. And it was on that day that the revolution began.

March eighth was International Woman's Day. The Social Democrats in Petrograd had intended to mark the day by issuing a few leaflets and declarations. No strikes had been called for that day. When the women workers in the textile factories threatened to strike, the Bolshevik Kayurov warned them against premature action. But the women were not to be held back. Getting the men who worked in the huge Putilov metalworks to join them, on March eighth they took to the streets. They formed processions carrying banners with the slogan *Down with the Autocracy* inscribed upon them, and they chanted "Give us bread!" as they marched somberly through the streets. When they attempted to invade the center of the city, the police tried to repel them, but they succeeded in reaching the Nevski Prospect anyhow. There were ninety thousand men and women on strike that day. Some of them reached the palaces of the Duma demanding bread, a hopeless request.

The day passed without any great incident, and the czarist authorities as well as the leftist leaders thought the demonstrations were over. But on the following day the number of people in the streets doubled. At least half of the industrial workers of Petrograd were now on strike. When the workers showed up at the factories on the morning of March ninth, they did not go to work. Instead they held meetings, then went out to support what was quickly developing into a general strike. When the workers marched down the Nevski Prospect, they found crowds of middle-class people cheering them on. The Cossacks had been called out by the government, but instead of charging the mass of people they simply walked their horses through them. Everywhere the crowd was heartened by the rumor that the Cossacks had promised not to shoot. Throughout the day huge crowds of people poured from one section of the city to another. The police broke them up continuously, and there were vicious battles. Toward the police, the "Pharaohs," the crowd showed only deep hatred. They threw stones, pieces of ice, anything at hand. And in these battles a remarkable thing was observed—not only did the Cossacks not interfere, they seemed to side with the workers! The crowd's enthusiasm was aroused by a report that when a policeman struck a woman with his club, the Cossacks rode the police down and drove them away. When the workers from the Erikson factory—some twenty-five hundred of them—ran into a Cossack squadron on the Sampsonievsky Prospect, the Cossacks rode gently through them. Kayurov, a Bolshevik worker, was there. "Some of them smiled," he recalled, "and one of them gave the workers a good wink."

The Cossacks even began to discuss matters with the workers milling around them. Their officers, now deeply alarmed, called back the patrol and lined it up across the street. But even this could not stop the disintegration. The Cossacks sat motionless while the workers dived under the bellies of their horses. What did this mean?

The Cossacks, those ancient subduers and punishers of the people, had always received special treatment at the hands of the czars. They were not peasants. They owned their own land, their own horses. And they enjoyed an almost autonomous self-government in their territories in the Ukraine and along the banks of the river Don. But they were as sick of war as anyone else. Above all they were sick of being pushed and pulled and always used to break the people. They wanted to go home. Therefore they winked. If the workers could pull it off, they would not stop them.

The military governor of Petrograd, Khabalov, had long since laid plans to deal with an uprising. On the first day, March eighth, he used police forces. On the second day, March ninth, he sent out the Cossacks. He held back infantry until events should develop further. It has been suggested that the police purposely displayed weakness during these days, hoping to lure the workers into a bloody showdown which would break their strength. If true, they badly miscalculated.

On March tenth the strike spread to include all of Petrograd. Now there were 240,000 workers in the streets. Students, lawyers, small businessmen joined them. Meetings were held in the open. Orators addressed the crowds from the Alexander III monument. The police opened fire. A speaker fell. Shots from the crowd killed a police inspector. Suddenly the Cossacks present fired a volley at the police, who immediately ran away. Kayurov reported how a group of workers were being whipped by mounted police within sight of a squadron of Cossacks. Kayurov and a few other workers walked over to the Cossacks, caps in hand, and said: "Brothers—Cossacks, help the workers in a struggle for their peaceable demands; you see how the Pharaohs treat us hungry workers. Help us!" The perfect psychology of this approach in humble supplication had its effect. "The Cossacks glanced at each other in some special way," Kayurov continued, "and we were hardly out of the way before they rushed into the fight." Almost immediately the police were dispersed. A Cossack who had cut down a police inspector with his sabre was tossed in the arms of the enraptured crowd.

Now the police began to go into hiding. There would be no mercy for them, and they knew it. The crowd could not compromise with them—if the revolution failed, these were the men who would be their executioners. Only death could settle the scores between people and police. In their place now appeared the infantry. They had established barricades across the most important streets. Toward them the crowd behaved cautiously, seeking by every means to win them over, not to antagonize them. In this the women workers had the greatest effect. After all, who were these soldiers but the brothers, husbands, and fathers of the Russian people themselves? The war had brought this about. The regiments stationed in Petrograd were not the professional soldiers of former days. Even the crack Guards regiments were full now of conscripts—peasant boys who had only recently been taken from their villages. Many of them had seen action at the front and would do anything to avoid returning there; others had seen how the autocracy had crushed their own families back home. And among them were drafted workers who had experience at political agitation. But when the people—led by women workers—approached them, cap in hand, to ask them why they obstructed the streets, these soldiers turned away sullenly. They were torn now between the terrible discipline of the army and the demands of the people. What if the revolution failed? Then the soldiers would be court-martialed and shot. They could expect no mercy from their officers. They had to be very careful. They would act only when they were convinced that the workers were in earnest—that they meant to go all the way and win the victory. As the crowds surged around them, arguing, begging, discussing, breaking into their ranks, the soldiers wavered. Perhaps they would remain neutral for a while—but no more. They were not yet ready to decide.

By this time the authorities in Petrograd realized that they were facing a full-scale revolution. They telegraphed the Czar, begging for instructions and for reinforcements from the front. But Nicholas tele-graphed Khabalov on March tenth: I ORDER THAT THE DISORDERS IN THE CAPITAL BE STOPPED TOMORROW. That is all. "I wish it, therefore it must be"—that was Nicholas' response. By this time, too, the revolutionary leaders in Petrograd had realized that the people were in earnest. They rushed to assume the leadership of the demonstration they had warned against. A three-day general strike was called by a committee consisting of Bolshevik, Menshevik, and Social Revolutionary lead-ers, united for once. Khabalov's reaction to this was to arrest about one hundred of these leaders and order the workers to return to their factories—not immedi-ately, but in three days, when the general strike would have ended anyhow. This was understood by the crowds as a sign of weakness.

By morning of March eleventh, police stations throughout the city had been wrecked. Police arms—revolvers and rifles and ammunition—were in the hands of the crowd. The hated Pharaohs had gone into hiding—those of them who had not been killed. March eleventh was a Sunday, and the factories, which had been the rallying centers of the workers, were closed. But they flocked once again to the streets.

When the bridges over the Neva were raised against them, they scrambled over the icy surface of the river. When they reached the center of the city, they found the troops had been ordered out in force against them. Today they had orders to shoot. And some of them did shoot—mainly the selected training squads of the regi-ments. It was now no longer possible for the soldiers to maintain a benevolent neutrality. Their officers or-dered them to shoot; the people begged them not to shoot their brothers and sisters. The pressure upon them had brought them to the breaking point. In one incident sixty workers were shot down by the soldiers.

Immediately workers rushed off to the barracks of the Pavlovsky Regiment. "Tell your comrades that your regiment too is shooting at us—we saw soldiers in your uniform. . . ." To the soldiers this came as a shameful reproach. By evening the fourth company of this regiment left under the orders of a noncommissioned officer, without permission, to round up its training squad which had fired on the people. On their way they had gun battles with remnants of the police.

When this company returned, they aroused the entire regiment. But suddenly it was discovered that their rifles had been removed by the officers. Then they found themselves surrounded by the Preobrazhensky Regiment. Nineteen of the mutinous soldiers were arrested. Later that night it was found that twenty-one others had previously given weapons to the people. These twenty-one men, who would certainly on the morrow face arrest if the revolution failed, now scurried off through the night to find allies among the other regiments in the city. In any event, debates were raging all night long in the soldiers' barracks throughout Petrograd.

Nor did the workers get much rest. The real crisis of the revolution was upon them now. They would either swing the regiments to their side or face disaster. But they retained confidence. At dawn on March twelfth a great mass of workers held a meeting just outside the gates of the compound in which were the barracks of the Moscow Regiment. They were scattered by machine-gun fire from guns operated by the officers. But the age-old appeal of workers to soldiers had at last been heard. While the workers were scattering before the guns of the Moscow Regiment the Volynsk Regiment mutinied. A sergeant, Timofeyev Kirpichnikov, seems to have been the moving spirit who first rallied his company and then the entire regiment to the revolution. Some of the officers were shot. Then the Volynsk men poured into the streets and began calling out the other regiments to join them. They marched in perfect order, their band playing as they went. Soon the Preobrazhensky Regiment, the Litovski Regiment, the Moscow Regiment all joined the revolution. In most cases the Czarist officers were shot or, ripping their epaulets from their shoulders, fled into hiding.

Armored cars bearing red revolutionary banners began to appear in the streets. Workers, armed with pistols taken from the police, would organize companies of soldiers and together storm police stations throughout Petrograd, which continued to hold out. Soon the workers faced the great Fortress of Peter and Paul. New field guns had been placed in its embrasures. Did the men inside intend to make a fight of it? No—after assurances that officers would not be killed the fortress surrendered to the revolutionaries. All Petrograd was now in their hands.

What had the czarist government been doing all this time? On this same March twelfth which saw the triumph of the revolution General Khabalov ordered posters proclaiming martial law plastered all over the city. Unfortunately, no glue could be found, or brushes with which to complete this task. And on this day, too, General Ivanov moved on Petrograd from the front with the famous Battalion of Saint George—crack and disciplined troops. He had been given dictatorial powers by Nicholas to crush the uprisings. When he reached Tsarskoe Selo on the outskirts of Petrograd, Ivanov sent a telegram to General Khabalov, who was now under siege in the Admiralty building. To Ivanov's inquiries as to how many troops remained loyal, what parts of the city were in rebel hands, and so forth, Khabalov was forced to reply, "I have at my disposal in the Admiralty building four companies of the

Guard, five squadrons of cavalry and Cossacks, and two batteries; the rest of the troops have gone over to the revolutionists. The whole city is in the hands of the revolutionists." Upon receiving this reply, General Ivanov turned back and gave up his attempt to enter Petrograd.

The inner meaning of this crumbling of czarist power is obvious. A state revolution affects the army just as deeply as it does the revolutionary masses for the simple reason that the army is composed of men from these same masses. The essence of a revolution is that no one will any longer obey the orders of the old government. So no glue was to be found, no brushes were available—who would, after all, go out and round up these simple supplies? When he issued his orders to the regiments in Petrograd to crush the revolution, Khabalov found, as he later put it: "The regiment starts, starts under a brave officer, but . . . there are no results." How can there be results when the soldiers of the regiments are only awaiting an opportunity to kill their officers and go over to the revolution? As for the police, the training squads, the officers, the "crack" battalions—these are so small a force that they simply vanish beneath the weight of the people's assault. The months and years following the revolution were to be filled with gallant colonels and generals who would say, "Give me one strong regiment and I'll soon put an end to all this mess." But where, in the midst of a revolution, will they ever find that one good regiment?

And what of the Czar and Czarina? They moved through this terrible week like sleepwalkers. The Czar refused to believe that anything serious was happening. When Mikhail Rodzianko, President of the Duma, himself terrified by the mass rising, telegraphed Nicholas that some sort of compromises would have to be made, Nicholas commented that he had received "some more rubbish from that fat Rodzianko." The Czarina Alix sent telegrams by the score to her husband—at first demanding firm action, reassuring him that a few hangings, a few regiments would soon restore order. But finally, when the city was in the hands of the revolutionists, even she admitted that some concessions would have to be made. Unfortunately, it was now too late for concessions. Nobody—not even the grand dukes, the Chiefs of Staff, the Duma—could tolerate another moment of Romanov rule. Certainly the people would not hear of it—and the others were too frightened to do anything but agree.

On March thirteenth Nicholas, now finally alarmed, set out in his private train to rejoin his family at Tsarskoe Selo. At first the journey went smoothly. But when the train reached the village of Visher, the railroad workers would not permit it to travel on. The train was rerouted by way of another line, but when it reached the Bologoe station, it was again stopped by the railroad men. The Czar was not to be permitted into Petrograd. As Trotsky observed, "With its simple railroad pawns, the revolution had cried 'check' to the king!" The wandering train finally had to double back to military headquarters at Pskov, where Nicholas awaited further word.

Meanwhile, the revolutionary regiments in Petrograd were marching with bands playing the "Marseillaise" to the Tauride Palace. This was the official meeting place of the national Duma and soon became the focus of the revolution. The Duma itself, which had spoken up so boldly for revolution in the past, was terrified of its actuality. Many of its members were in hiding; others surveyed events with despair. The liberals, the Cadet party, saw in the revolution only chaos and a threat to their own positions. Most of them hoped to be able to preserve at least the principle of constitutional monarchy. Nicholas would abdicate—but the throne would descend to his son, or possibly to one of the grand dukes. Nicholas' son was certainly too ill to be parted from his family, and the grand dukes wisely declined invitations to assume the throne, but in any event the people would never have accepted any such solution. For the regiments and crowds which moved to the Tauride Palace were not going there to support the Duma—they were going there to set up a new soviet, just as they had done in 1905.

The soviet grew out of the strike committees of the workers, the leadership of the regiments, those few socialist leaders who were not in exile (the jails had already been emptied by the crowds, and some political leaders were thus set free, along with criminals of all kinds), and, in fact, anyone bold enough or talkative enough to assume importance. While the Duma was setting up a special committee under the leadership of Paul Milyukov, Mikhail Rodzianko, and Alexander Guchkov to try to sort some order out of events, in another wing of the Tauride Palace a soviet was being established by Bolsheviks, Mensheviks, and Social Revolutionaries. Soon it was plain that only the orders of this soviet would be obeyed by the soldiers and workers—they had almost no confidence in the Duma, which they suspected (correctly) of attempting to preserve some elements of the old order.

By evening on March twelfth the Soviet had already appointed a special Executive Committee and commissions to handle such problems as food and military affairs. There were more than a hundred members of this soviet—deputies elected by the workers' strike committees and the soldiers—and if their meetings were chaotic, there was certainly an air of elation and brotherhood about them. Differences that had split the socialist movement in the past were now forgotten—at least temporarily—as the Soviet got down to the business of governing. N. N. Sukhanov, a Menshevik who was on the Soviet's Executive Committee, has described one of the early meetings of the Soviet: "Standing on stools, their rifles in their hands, agitated and stuttering, straining all their powers to give a concentrated account of the messages that had been given to them . . . one after another the soldiers' deputies told of what had been happening in their companies. Their stories were artless and repeated each other almost word for word. The audience listened as children listen to a wonderful enthralling fairy tale they know by heart, holding their breaths, with craning necks and unseeing eyes . . . 'we had a meeting . . . we've been told to say . . . that we refuse to serve against the people any more, we're going to join with our brother workers . . . we would lay down our lives for that.' It was then and there proposed, and approved with storms of applause, to fuse together the revolutionary army and the proletariat of the capitol, and create a united organization to be called from then on the 'Soviet of Workers' and Soldiers' Deputies.' "

Before the evident power of the Soviet the Duma leadership's plans to preserve some element of monarchy quickly crumbled. Delegates were sent from the Duma to Nicholas at Pskov with instructions to secure an abdication. And in the meantime, the generals commanding Russian armies at the front had taken a straw vote among themselves. They found they were unanimously terrified of the revolution, that they could not count on their troops to put it down, and that the Czar's only recourse would be to abdicate. So, on the night of March fifteenth, Nicholas II signed the abdication brought to him by the Duma delegates. "In agreement with the Imperial Duma, we have thought it good to abdicate from the throne of the Russian State, and to lay down the supreme power. . . ." The Czar ended the document "May the Lord God help Russia!" Later that night he was to confide to his diary (with considerable justification): "At 1 o'clock in the morning I left Pskov with heavy feelings; around me treason, cowardice, deceit." Within a few days the royal train reached Tsarskoe Selo at last. There Nicholas rejoined the Czarina Alix and his family. They were all placed under house arrest and confined to the palace.

A brief attempt on the part of the Duma to get one of the grand dukes to assume the Russian throne came to nothing, and, for the first time since Ivan the Terrible assumed the title in 1547, there was no czar in Russia. Arriving exhausted at Tsarskoe Selo, Nicholas had said simply, "There is no justice among men." But the generations of untold millions of suffering serfs, peasants, workers, and soldiers would not have agreed with him.

CHAPTER FIVE

Power and Paradox

ON MARCH 16, 1917, when Petrograd at last drew breath and looked around, it was seen that the revolution, completely successful, had cost comparatively few casualties and little damage. A little over one thousand workers and soldiers lay dead, buildings were scarred by bullet marks, windows were smashed, certain establishments such as the police stations were utterly wrecked, but in general the city presented a remarkably calm outer appearance considering what it had gone through. The Romanov dynasty was gone; gone, too, the symbols of its power, the hated police, the political prisons, the repressions—even the portraits of the Czar and certain monuments to former czars had been destroyed. There had been little looting, however. It was usually only necessary for someone in the mob to remind it that they were dealing now with property which would belong to all the people for looting and burning to cease.

Over the Czar's Winter Palace floated a huge red banner. Yet beneath the apparently peaceful surface of the city a bitter struggle was developing.

Within the Tauride Palace there now existed the Provisional Government, formed by the Duma and led by the Cadets and other liberal and conservative parties, and the soviet of Workers' and Soldiers' Deputies, formed by the masses and led by Bolsheviks, Mensheviks, and Social Revolutionaries. Although these two groups patched up an agreement during their first days of power, it soon became obvious that they constituted two separate governments with conflicting aims. The Provisional Government led by its dynamic foreign minister, the Cadet leader Paul Milyukov, and including just one socialist—the young lawyer Alexander Kerensky—devoted all of its resources to getting things back to normal, restraining the revolutionary impulses of the people and, above all, continuing the war against Germany. With intimate connections to the English, French, and American embassies, and commitments, both emotional and financial, to an Allied victory, the Provisional Government saw as its prime task the revitalizing of the army and the waging of war to the death against the Kaiser. They did not abandon the czarist war aims, either—the conquest of Constantinople, the heavy reparations, and so on. Czarist Russia had been bound to the Allies by secret treaties which promised her large spoils in case of victory. The Provisional Government intended to honor these treaties.

The Soviet, on the other hand, was primarily concerned to reap immediately the benefits of the revolution. It called for an eight-hour day, immediate land distribution, democratization of the army, denunciation of the czarist secret treaties, and a negotiated peace. But within the Soviet there were deep differences as to how these aims were to be achieved. The power the Soviet had won soon exposed its members to the terrible difficulties any Russian government had to face. The demand for an eight-hour day, for example, was countered by the soldiers, who wanted to know why they should have to fight and suffer twenty-four hours a day at the front while workers toiled only eight hours a day in Petrograd. Under the circumstances the eight-hour day was given only lip service. Land distribution presented yet another set of problems. In many areas the peasants were already seizing the land. But much of the land belonged to just that class of people represented by the Provisional Government. They would certainly not surrender it without a fight, which would mean civil war.

The issue of the army—which meant the issue of war or peace—was a knotty one. If peace were to be bought at any price, that price might well be the revolution itself. With the army demoralized, what was to prevent the Kaiser from marching on Petrograd and restoring the Czar to the throne? If Russia denounced the secret treaties, would not the Allies abandon her —even, perhaps, intervene with troops to strangle the revolution? Under the circumstances it was decided that the army would have to adopt a defensist policy. That is, they would make no attacks, indulge in no offensives. They would remain in their lines but would resist any attempted advance on the part of the Germans. Meantime, although the Allies could count on Russian support, the Soviet would issue a call to all the peoples of the world to make immediate peace without revenge. But the Allies ignored the Soviet appeal for a peace conference.

That both these programs were weak, in fact self-contradictory, is quite evident. The question of war and peace, the question of land—these were matters which would be settled by the soldiers and the peasants no matter what policy was decided upon by either Provisional Government or Soviet. Already Russian troops were beginning to desert by the hundreds of thousands. In many areas of the front they fraternized freely with the Germans. For them the war was over, no matter what the politicians said. Peasant soldiers wanted to hurry home to share in the distribution of land, and nothing was going to stop them. On the other hand, the officers and certain of the divisions on the southern front which had won great victories over the Austrians felt very strongly that they must fight on simply to defend their revolution against the Kaiser.

The inner meaning of this dual power which existed in the Tauride Palace was quite simply that it reflected class interests which had not yet been resolved by the first revolution. The Mensheviks, with a commanding majority in the Soviet, were afraid to assume complete power. As always, they feared they would not be able to run the vast and intricate government establishment —for that they felt they needed the educated middle classes and the Provisional Government. Besides that, it had long been Menshevik theory that a long-term development of capitalist democracy was necessary in Russia before any socialist take-over. The Provisional Government, on the other hand, which had been terrified by events and which knew it had to depend on the sufferance of the Soviet to make any decision stick, felt itself too weak to take vigorous action.

Compromise was the result. While real power rested with the Soviet, the administration of the country was left to the Provisional Government. Since neither institution could afford to do without the other, they compromised their programs until it seemed that neither had any program at all.

And now reports began to pour in from all over Russia—reports of successful uprisings in Moscow, Kiev, Minsk—of revolution sweeping the provisional towns and districts. Local Soviets were formed throughout the land, and all of these were willing to follow the lead of the Petrograd Soviet in allowing the Provisional Government to retain power. But unless the problems of food, land, and peace were solved quickly, it was questionable how long the country would submit to Petrograd. Already the pressure of the soldiers in the Soviet had resulted in the famous order Number One.

Order Number One, passed by the Soviet during the hottest moments of its earliest meetings, provided for the complete reorganization of the army. From now on officers would have to be polite to their men, off-duty salutes were abolished, all units were to organize their own committees of soldiers to control weapons, all units were to consider themselves under the direct orders of the Soviet, obeying Provisional Government orders only where they did not contradict Soviet orders. Officers were to be elected by the men. The Provisional Government could do nothing but accept this order, hoping the day was not far off when it could be rescinded.

As the only socialist in the Provisional Government, Alexander Kerensky now began to assume some importance. Whenever knotty problems had to be resolved with the Soviet, Kerensky seemed the logical errand boy. Both sides made use of him in this respect. But he had a certain force of his own as well. He was young, attractive, and had great oratorical gifts. He was a born actor who could throw his emotions into a political speech with rousing effect. He soon became a favorite with the crowds who clustered outside the Tauride Palace. His socialism did not run very deep; nor, for that matter, did his liberalism. He was, first of all, an opportunist with dreams of personal glory and power. He had been born and raised in Simbirsk, Lenin's home town; in fact, Lenin had attended the school run by Kerensky's father. But the differences between these two could not have been greater.

The era of compromise, of uneasy dual power, was Kerensky's golden chance to shine. When men are unwilling to support their deepest convictions, through fear or policy, then the histrionic abilities of a political demagogue have their greatest opportunity.

Sukhanov relates how one day in the Tauride Palace shots were heard. Immediately someone raised the cry "Cossacks!" "Kerensky," Sukhanov says, "rushed to the window, leaped on the sill, and sticking his head out shouted in a hoarse, broken voice: 'Stations everyone! Defend the Duma! Listen to me—I, Kerensky, am speaking to you, Kerensky is speaking to you! Defend your freedom and the revolution, defend the Duma! Stations everyone!' . . . It was clear that the shots were accidental—most probably from the inexperienced hands of some workers handling a rifle for the first time. It was ridiculous and a little embarrassing. I went over to Kerensky. 'Everything's all right,' I said in a low voice . . . Kerensky broke into a rage and began bellowing at me, shakily picking his words, 'I demand—that everyone—do his duty—and not interfere—when I—give orders!' "

Despite the popularity of Kerensky, the Provisional Government knew it had little support at home, and it rejoiced when the Allied governments hurried to give it formal recognition. The United States was the first country to recognize the Provisional Government as Russia's legal government. The revolution had enjoyed tremendous support among the American people and was welcomed by Woodrow Wilson and his Cabinet. Now, as he led America into the First World War, it seemed as if, with the end of czardom, it was truly a war to make the world safe for democracy. The American Ambassador in Petrograd, a plain-spoken and clear-thinking midwestern businessman named David R. Francis, hurried to give the new government every support. He helped to get loans from the United States which were to total $325 million to prop up the Provisional Government. French and English recognition soon followed.

The Allies embarked on a policy of keeping Russia in the war at all costs. For this reason they supported the Provisional Government in every way they could in its struggle with the Soviet, which, the Allies suspected, would take Russia out of the war.

The war was the rock on which policy continually foundered. The vast masses of Russia wanted peace. But neither Provisional Government nor Soviet could give them peace, each for its own reasons. And upon the fact of war, all domestic reforms crumbled. The eight-hour day, land distribution, freedom of the press were all victims of the needs of war. Besides that, the terrible food shortage caused by the war continued unrelenting to plague the authorities.

But in these early days of revolutionary victory the brotherhood of the people, no matter what their political beliefs, was still a potent force. On April fifth a huge public funeral was given to the workers and soldiers who had fallen during the uprising. And in this solemn event all the people joined—students, businessmen, politicians, officers, bureaucrats, the middle classes joined the workers and soldiers as they marched, a million strong, to the recently dug mass grave on Mars Field in Petrograd. From all the workers' district the coffins streamed in—all painted red and borne on the shoulders of fathers, brothers, and sons. At one-minute intervals the great guns of the Peter and Paul fortress boomed over the city in salute. Red banners floated everywhere over the crowd: Onlookers remarked on the perfect order the people maintained without the need of police, and the great silence in which only the trudging of millions of feet could be heard. It was one of those moments in the life of a great nation when the people seem lifted above themselves, seem to express in their quiet solidarity the essential brotherhood of all men.

And yet, behind the facade of the dual government, behind the endless arguments of politicians, a decisive struggle was developing. The worker, the peasant, the soldier all said, "Give us peace, give us reform, give us land." But the Soviet could only reply, "Wait." The people were not in the mood to wait long. And now they were to find a voice, a leader, and a program. On April 16, 1917, Lenin returned to Petrograd and set in motion those events which were eventually to change the name of the city to Leningrad.

The exiles—Plekhanov, Lenin, Trotsky, Martov, Dan, and the rest—had watched the revolution in stunned surprise from abroad. Now they all scrambled to get home as soon as possible. Those among them who supported the war, such as Plekhanov and Dan and other Mensheviks, found their pathway cleared by the Allied governments and hurried to take their places in the new Soviet. But for Lenin and Trotsky and their followers it was different. These men had openly and continuously denounced the war and demanded Russian withdrawal from it. The Allied governments considered them altogether too dangerous to admit back into Russia. Trotsky, who had spent a few months editing a Russian-language newspaper in Brooklyn, took ship to Petrograd only to be forcibly removed by British authorities in Halifax and held by them for four weeks in custody. Lenin, however, found another way to return.

Lenin had only been able to follow events in Russia through the foreign press. But even in exile in Switzerland he had instantly seen the paradoxes behind the new government. This Provisional Government and its Soviet supporters, Lenin wrote in *Pravda* (the Bolshevik newspaper in Petrograd), could never hope to give the people peace, bread, and land, because to do so would entail a fight against the industrialists and landlords who composed the Provisional Government. The only answer was for the people of Russia to organize behind the Petrograd Soviet and bend it to their will. A "People's Militia" should be formed to take the place of the police; the Soviet should openly repudiate all the czarist treaties with the Allies and seek an immediate armistice with Germany; it must work for the liberation of all the subject peoples in Russia; it must issue a summons to the workers of every country to end the war by revolution; the national debt piled up by czarist governments must be renounced. In these "Letters from Afar," Lenin renewed his grip on the lower echelons of the Bolshevik movement inside Russia.

But meantime he was growing desperately impatient to make his way somehow to Petrograd and assume his rightful place. The other exiles in Switzerland argued endlessly over such matters as disguises. At one point it was proposed that Lenin would pretend to be a

123

deaf-mute Swede. But Krupskaya warned him: "You'll fall asleep and see Mensheviks in your dreams and you'll start swearing and shouting, 'Scoundrels, scoundrels!' and give the whole plot away." But all roads to Russia seemed to lead through Germany, an enemy country.

The Kaiser's government had welcomed the Russian Revolution because in it they foresaw the end of Russian war efforts. German agents had been active in distributing funds (under deep cover) to all the revolutionary parties on the simple principle of keeping as much trouble brewing in an enemy country as possible. In this financing of revolutionary groups German agents were doing no more than agents of any wartime government in backing those who would presumably bring them some benefit. For the most part, the revolutionary parties concerned were not aware that the money came from Germany (or other foreign sources) and in any event they were not "selling" anything for it. They had their revolutionary programs, which they intended to carry out with or without clandestine German (or American, British, or French) support. And in assuming that this revolutionary activity would benefit them, the Kaiser's government made one of its many huge blunders. This is a matter we will go into later—for the moment it is enough to say that the German government hoped that Lenin's return to Russia would bring about an eventual collapse in the war effort. When, therefore, Martov and a few other of the Russian exiles thought up a scheme whereby they would travel across Germany in a sealed train, the German government accepted it gladly. As Winston Churchill was later to express it: ". . . it was with a sense of awe that they [the Germans] turned upon Russia the most grisly of all weapons. They transported Lenin in a sealed truck like a plague bacillus from Switzerland into Russia."

Lenin was nearly forty-seven years old at this time. His life with Krupskaya in Zurich had been peaceful —full of days in the library, long walks in the woods, and, always, innumerable letters and pamphlets. But now he was eager to get into the thick of the fighting. In various devious ways negotiations were opened with German agents. There was much argument back and forth, but agreement was finally reached on the main points. Lenin and his associates would be carried across Germany in a sealed train by the German government. On Lenin's insistence no German was to be permitted on the train, no talks of any kind were to be held.

Finally, on April ninth, the train was ready. With about thirty Russian exiles aboard, including Lenin and Krupskaya, it pulled out of Zurich. There was a scene at the railroad station when some of the Russian socialists begged their comrades not to go as guests of the German government, thereby opening themselves to charges of treason. But Lenin was firmly resolved. When he entered his compartment, he found a man suspected of being a German spy seated there. Without a word or a change of expression Lenin picked up the man by his collar and tossed him back onto the platform.

The trip through Germany was uneventful. When a German socialist asked to meet Lenin and the others, he was refused admittance. Lenin himself appears to have been convinced that they would all be arrested as soon as they reached Petrograd. In Sweden Lenin was talked into buying himself a new pair of shoes. He refused to buy a new overcoat, however, declaring that he was not returning to Russia to open a tailor's shop. When the party reached Finland, Krupskaya recalled, "everything was already familiar and dear to us: the wretched third-class cars, the Russian soldiers. It was terribly good."

When Lenin's train arrived late on the night of April sixteenth at Petrograd's shabby Finland Station, Bolsheviks and representatives of both the Provisional Government and the Soviet were there to greet him. Behind them, in the darkness which was illuminated by searchlights, stood vast thousands of the people. Sukhanov was there and described the scene. Lenin came walking into the station almost at a run. His coat was unbuttoned, and he looked cold. He was carrying a huge bouquet of roses which someone had thrust into his hand. Running through the room, he almost crashed into Nicholas Chkheidze, the Menshevik President of the Petrograd Soviet—a political enemy who appeared none too happy to have to welcome Lenin to the city. "Comrade Lenin," Chkheidze said in his carefully oratorical speech of greeting, "in the name of the Petrograd Soviet and of the whole revolution, we welcome you to Russia . . . but we consider that at the present time the principal task of the revolutionary democracy is to defend our revolution against every kind of attack, both from within and from without. . . . We hope that you will join us in striving toward this goal." Lenin, according to Sukhanov, stood there, "looking as if all this that was happening only a few feet away did not concern him in the least; he glanced from one side to the other; looked over the surrounding public, and even examined the ceiling . . . while rearranging his bouquet (which harmonized rather badly with his whole figure)." When Chkheidze finished, Lenin turned to the crowd and replied: "Dear comrades, soldiers, sailors and workers, I am happy to greet in you the victorious Russian revolution, to greet you as the advance guard of the international proletarian army.

. . . The war of imperialist brigandage is the beginning of civil war in Europe. . . . The hour is not far when . . . the people will turn their arms against their capitalist exploiters. . . . Long live the International Social Revolution!"

"Suddenly," Sukhanov relates, "before the eyes of all of us, completely swallowed up by the routine drudgery of the revolution, there was presented a bright, blinding, exotic light . . . Lenin's voice, heard straight from the train, was a "voice from outside." There had broken in upon us in the revolution a note that was . . . novel, harsh and somewhat deafening."

Lenin hurried from the room. Outside he found, to his great surprise, a file of sailors who presented arms in salute. Huge crowds roared for him, the searchlight played over great red banners and bands crashed out the "Marseillaise." The crowd carried Lenin on their shoulders and deposited him atop one of the armored cars. With the spotlights of the Peter and Paul fortress shining on him, Lenin's car proceeded through the crowded streets at the head of what had become an immense procession from the station. The bands played, the people cheered wildly, and Lenin had to speak several times to the crowds. Always his theme was the ending of the war through international socialist revolution. And when finally the procession reached the palace of Kshesinskaya (a prima ballerina who had been one of the Czar's favorites), which had been taken over for Bolshevik Party headquarters, the crowds refused to disperse until Lenin had spoken to them twice more from the balcony.

Inside the palace the Bolshevik dignitaries unleashed long speeches of welcome. Lenin, says Trotsky, endured them like a pedestrian waiting in a doorway for the rain to stop. Finally he rose to speak and kept the floor for two hours. What he had to say filled his followers with consternation. "On the journey here with my comrades," he said, "I was expecting that they would take us straight from the station to Peter and Paul. We are far from that, it seems. But let us not give up the hope that we shall still not escape that experience." He denounced the Provisional Government, swept aside the Soviet proposals for reforms, and gave those Bolsheviks who had supported the Soviet (Stalin was one) a tongue-lashing. "We don't need any parliamentary republic. We don't need any bourgeois democracy. We don't need any government except the Soviet of Workers', Soldiers', and Peasants' Deputies!"

Lenin's savage assault on his fellow party members was not very unusual. He had long since made of the Bolshevik Party a tightly disciplined, dictatorially organized group. Although debate was permitted within the various committees of the party, once a vote was taken and a decision reached, all members of the committee were expected to adhere to the decision and carry it out wholeheartedly. A practice was even made of assigning to carry out decisions of the committee those members who had opposed them, thus testing their loyalty and implicating them in the results as deeply as those who had favored the decision. And committees at lower levels of the party organization were expected to carry out without question decisions reached by committees at higher levels. Highest of all was the Central Committee of the party—the group to which Lenin was now addressing himself. Since there was no escape from a final decision of the Central Committee once that decision was taken, Lenin's harangue, like most debates and speeches before the Central Committee, was violent, long, and ruthless in tone. Lenin and the other Bolsheviks often tended to adopt this same imperious tone when addressing themselves to those who were outside the Bolshevik party, usually with the effect of enraging their audience. And when this dictatorial manner, this antidemocratic procedure were brought to bear on national problems in later years, disaster was to follow. It was in large part because of their experience with and realization of the antidemocratic nature of the Bolshevik party organization that many non-Bolshevik socialists trembled at the prospects of a Bolshevik seizure of power. The future was to prove those fears correct.

Sukhanov, who had sneaked into the meeting, was appalled by its tone. He relates that he staggered out onto the street after Lenin's brutal speech "feeling as if I had been flogged over the head with a flail. Only one thing was clear: there was no way for me, a nonparty man, to go along with Lenin." A Bolshevik naval officer who had been present wrote: "The words of Ilyich laid down a Rubicon between the tactics of yesterday and today."

The more conservative party members such as Stalin and Lev Kamenev (who were editing *Pravda*) had been moving closer and closer to positions which were almost identical to those of the Mensheviks. It even seemed likely that the Social Democratic Party might unite once again. To the Bolsheviks, Lenin's words (which soon became known as his "April Theses") sounded like madness. Immersed in the details of the revolution, the Bolsheviks had thought they would need years of organization and propaganda before attempting to seize power. Here was Lenin urging them to fight for socialism at once, do away with the liberal Provisional Government, and establish a dictatorship of the workers expressed through the Soviet. For several weeks it appeared that Lenin was isolated within his own party.

But Lenin's demands were overwhelmingly appealing to the mass of the people. And many of the leaders of this mass—the strike committeemen, the soldiers' deputies, the women delegates to the various conferences—were of that grim and dedicated lower layer of Bolsheviks who had fought hard for the revolution while the leadership of the party hesitated. It was to this group that Lenin addressed himself—and they responded. In a situation in which politicians seemed to change their beliefs from day to day, in which rumor and fear could sweep the streets at any moment, in which, above all, nothing seemed to have changed for the masses in spite of the revolution, Lenin's voice, his strict adherence to principles, made a great appeal. Added to this was his readiness to compromise theory where events showed it to be wrong. He was above all a very practical man, and this too appealed to the people. Within a month the Bolsheviks had adopted his new ideas as their own and prepared to carry them out.

Thus by the end of April there existed in Petrograd not only a Provisional Government with almost no real power and a Soviet with almost no direction, but also a third force—Lenin and his Bolsheviks. In the arena of revolutionary struggle these three eyed each other warily while each planned against the other two. Days of dramatic conflict lay ahead.

CHAPTER SIX

Plot and Counterplot

IN THE CONFUSING PATTERN of events which was to lead to the Bolshevik revolution, a definite rhythm can be felt. While plots and counterplots rippled the surface of events in Petrograd, the deeper tides of mass feeling dictated the basic movements. It was Lenin's ability to gauge these deeper currents which eventually won him the victory.

Russian history has classified the events of spring and summer 1917 under the headings the April Days, the June Demonstrations, the July Days, and the counterrevolution. But these artificial titles merely hide the continuous ebb and flow of popular political opinion at the same time they help define it.

The Russian people remained at all times considerably to the left of their political leadership. Their patience had limits. Thus, during the April Days, the people surged into the streets to warn the Soviet that they would no longer tolerate the foreign policy of the Provisional Government. The June Demonstrations were a test of strength among the socialist parties. The July Days were an ill-timed and premature series of street clashes in which Bolsheviks suffered a heavy defeat. The counterrevolution was the direct reaction of czarist and middle-class forces to the Bolshevik attempt in July.

But while the political pendulum swung from one extreme to the other, it must never be forgotten that the masses were learning from events. This was reflected in the elections of representatives from factory and regiment to local congresses and soviets which were continuously taking place. All during the turbulent summer of 1917 more and more Bolsheviks were elected. But at any given moment during this time the National Soviet deputies actually sitting at the Tauride Palace represented a slight lag in opinion because of the simple, practical fact that they could not be replaced as quickly as mass opinion changed.

The first crisis, the April Days (which took place in May by our calendar), was brought about by Milyukov, the Provisional Government's foreign minister and the leader of the liberal Cadet party. On May first he sent a note to the various Allied governments in which he promised that Russia would fight on to the end and that she would stick to the spirit and letter of the treaties which bound the Allies together. This meant that Russia would insist on such czarist schemes as the seizure of Constantinople, the division of Armenia, the grabbing of part of Persia. The people, who wanted peace above all else, would never stand for such war aims, and the Soviet knew it.

After Milyukov's note was published in the Petrograd newspapers (with angry editorial comment), the Soviet demanded that it be modified and clarified. Kerensky hurried to explain that the note presented merely "[Milyukov's] personal opinion." But it was hard for the people to see a difference between Milyukov's personal opinion and the policy of the foreign ministry of which he was head.

Why did Milyukov, an astute politician, offer this public affront to the Soviet? Partly because Russia badly needed loans from the Allied governments but partly also because he misgauged the temper of the people. A few days before he sent off his note a giant demonstration of war cripples and invalids had taken place in Petrograd. Armless, legless, mutilated veterans marched through the streets in hideous phalanxes, bearing banners demanding war to end. These men, crippled by the war, were bitterly demanding that their sacrifices should not have been in vain.

A few days later a large demonstration of students, officials, officers, and middle-class citizens was held on the Nevski Prospect; support for the Provisional Government and continued support for the war effort were the main themes.

As soon as the contents of the note to the Allies became clear to the people they once again took to the streets in gigantic demonstrations. The April Days had begun. Workers and peasants marched on the Tauride Palace with banners demanding *Down with Milyukov*. This demonstration was spontaneous. None of the socialist parties had called it forth, and the Soviet viewed it with alarm. The Menshevik and Social Revolutionary leaders of that body feared that the masses would bring about the downfall of the Provisional Government and force the power into the hands of the Soviet.

Meantime the workers and the regiments of soldiers were marching, and their mood was determined. A journalist present described the procession: "About a hundred armed men marched in front; after them solid phalanxes of unarmed men and women, a thousand strong. Living chains on both sides. Songs. Their faces amazed me. All those thousands had but one face, the stunned ecstatic face of the early Christian monks. Implacable, pitiless, ready for murder, inquisition, and death." But this frightening mass did not demand the downfall of the Provisional Government. They simply demanded that it respond to their wishes. The Central Committee of the Bolshevik party declared: "The motto 'Down with the Provisional Government' is incorrect at present because without a solid majority on the side of the revolutionary proletariat, such a motto is either an empty phrase or leads to attempts of an adventurous character."

On May third the Finland Regiment, accompanied by twenty-five thousand workers, appeared before the Tauride Palace to demand Milyukov's removal and that of Alexander Guchkov, the war minister. And although the Soviet feared to disturb the Provisional Government, it was now clear that some action would have to be taken. Accordingly a new Provisional Government excluding Milyukov, Guchkov, and several other of the most detested ministers was formed. Six socialists were now appointed to form, with the ten remaining liberal leaders, a new cabinet. The note to the Allies was disavowed, and an uneasy peace returned to the streets of the capital, thus bringing to a close the April Days.

The masses had spontaneously forced their Soviet to

take an important hand in directly governing the country. But in doing so, they had also placed the Mensheviks and Social Revolutionaries in the position of accepting responsibility for the government's policy —and this played directly into Lenin's hands. For the new coalition government brought the moderate socialists directly into the line of fire of Bolshevik propaganda.

On May seventeenth Trotsky, who had finally been released by the British, made his way back to Petrograd. Although he had not been a member of the Bolshevik party, he soon found that his opinions closely reflected those of Lenin, and after a few weeks he became a Bolshevik. His presence in Petrograd was to prove fully as important as Lenin's during the days ahead.

The new coalition government soon demonstrated that in the matter of war or peace it did not fundamentally differ with the previous government. Under pressure from the Allies, the coalition government decided that Russia must undertake an offensive. Kerensky was dispatched to the front to rouse the troops to fight— for the revolution now, instead of the Czar. But was this not the very revolution which had promised them peace? The soldiers now began to identify the socialist members of the coalition government with the old policy of war to the bitter end. Bolshevik agitators had a field day among the regiments.

Nor could the shattered Russian armies gather together the strength for any kind of decisive action. Desertions continued, chaos reigned in the chain of command; the generals were the same incompetents who had served the Czar—and the supply situation had, if anything, deteriorated during the winter. To order these armies to attack was only inviting disaster. And now, with Mensheviks and Social Revolutionaries joining the liberals in demanding an offensive, only the Bolsheviks stood out as the party who would bring peace.

In the middle of June a first All-Russian Congress of representatives of local soviets met at Petrograd. Although the Bolsheviks were heavily outnumbered by Mensheviks and Social Revolutionaries, they felt a growing confidence in their influence among the masses. When Irakli Tseretelli, the Menshevik leader who was also Minister of Posts and Telegraphs, addressed the All-Russian Congress, he declared: "There is no political party in Russia which would at the present time say 'Give us power.'"

Lenin, seated among the deputies, shouted out: "There is!"

A ripple of laughter spread through the hall, and when Lenin arose to speak, he returned to the point. "The citizen Minister of Posts and Telegraphs has declared that there is no political party in Russia that would agree to take the entire power on itself. I answer: there is. No party can refuse to do this, all parties are contending and must contend for the power, and our party will not refuse it. It is ready at any moment to take over the government."

Lenin's confidence was based on the steady swing of the workers and soldiers in Petrograd to the Bolshevik program. Ever since the Bolsheviks had been converted to Lenin's "April Theses," they had carried on an intensive and unremitting campaign among the factory committees and the regiments. Their progress was dramatically demonstrated only a week later.

The government's announcement of a new offensive was creating greater and greater unrest among the masses in Petrograd. If a few regiments at the front and the local soviets of some of the provincial cities still supported the idea of waging renewed war on behalf of the revolution, the workers of the capital saw in the new offensive only a betrayal of the revolution. Thinking to take advantage of this feeling, and also to demonstrate their rising strength, the Bolsheviks decided to call for demonstrations at the end of June. This was the genesis of the June Demonstrations. The people were to carry banners bearing the Bolshevik slogans: *Down with the ten capitalist ministers!, All power to the soviets!,* and *Bread, Peace and Freedom!* But when the more conservative socialists in the Soviet learned of the Bolshevik plans, they demanded that the demonstration be called off. It was too dangerous, they declared—it might lead to the downfall of the coalition government. In the face of these demands the Bolsheviks backed down and called off their demonstration. Seeking to press their advantage, the socialists of the Soviet decided to call a demonstration of their own. Tseretelli declared to the Bolshevik deputies: "Now we shall have an open and honest review of the revolutionary forces. . . . Now we shall see whom the majority is following, you or us."

The line of march was to duplicate that of the funeral march two months earlier—through the city and out to Mars Field. Four hundred thousand workers appeared on the streets in orderly groups and bearing placards and banners. They were awaited at Mars Field by the socialist leaders of the Soviet and by the delegates to the All-Russian Soviet Congress. There on the reviewing stand, as the workers and soldiers marched into Mars Field by the thousands, their leaders counted up the slogans. Gradually, to their horror, they found that the overwhelming majority of banners and placards read *Down with the ten capitalist ministers!* and *All power to the soviets!* Bolshevik slogans floated everywhere over the masses of workers and soldiers.

"Here and there," Sukhanov observed, "the chain of Bolshevik banners and columns would be broken by specifically Social Revolutionary or official Soviet slogans. But these were drowned in the mass." Face to face with the Petrograd workers, the Soviet leaders found that they had been won over to Bolshevism. The delegates to the Soviet Congress were frightened by the demonstration. As they looked out over Mars Field they reminded the Bolsheviks present that though they seemed to have won control in Petrograd, the army and the provinces remained aloof. Petrograd could not go against the entire country. The country's turn would soon come, the Bolsheviks replied. The June Demonstrations had clearly been a Bolshevik victory.

Meanwhile, the Russian offensive got under way. On June twenty-ninth, under cover of a barrage from thirteen hundred guns, thirty-one Russian divisions advanced against the Germans and Austrians. For the first few days things appeared to be going well. Kerensky reported to the Provisional Government from the front: "Today is the great triumph of the revolution. On June eighteenth, the Russian revolutionary army with colossal enthusiasm assumed the offensive." But within two weeks the offensive ground to a halt. On July sixteenth the Germans launched their counterattack, and the entire Russian front began to break up. Disaster overtook regiments, divisions, entire armies. The Germans advanced almost without opposition. It was perfectly clear that, revolutionary or not, the Russian army had ceased to exist as a fighting force. And its defeats during July 1917 led indirectly to new uprisings in Petrograd.

Bolshevik historians have always insisted that the attempted revolution in July—called the July Days—was spontaneous. The Bolsheviks claim to have argued *against* the pouring of people into the streets, the maneuvers of the regiments. Trotsky insists that the Bolshevik leadership knew that the time was not yet ripe. He points to the fact that the revolutionary impulses in Petrograd were much more advanced than those in the rest of the country, that any attempt to overthrow the Provisional Government would have isolated Petrograd and led to a losing civil war. Only after the people could no longer be restrained, after the regiments were already marching on the Tauride Palace, did the Bolshevik leadership assume reluctant command of the rising and attempt to divert it into peaceful channels. That, at least, is the official view. There exists much evidence, however, that if the Bolshevik high command—Lenin, Trotsky, Kamenev, Stalin, and the others—were against the movement, those lower echelons of Bolshevik leadership in the factories and regiments who had followed Lenin's "April Theses" were active from the very beginning in attempting to rouse the city.

As in April, it was the liberal Cadet party itself which ignited the July Days. The news of Russian disasters at the front had not been officially admitted by the Provisional Government, but they could not be kept secret much longer. Fearing the consequences of the news, the Cadet ministers in the government resigned in a body, leaving their socialist colleagues to collect the blame for the military defeats. It was the news of this mass resignation which set off an angry public outburst which became known as the July Days.

The First Machine-Gun Regiment, which because of its automatic weapons was the object of very special attention on the part of the Bolsheviks, acted first. On July sixteenth the Bolsheviks sent delegates to the regiments and factories, asking the soldiers and workers to join them in forcing their demands on the Provisional Government. Soon tens of thousands of people had taken to the streets. Led by armed regiments (among which now, for the first time, specially trained elements of the Red Guard—a sort of workers' militia—appeared), the mobs advanced on the Tauride Palace. Their demand was: All power to the soviets. They wanted to force the Soviet leadership to do away with the Provisional Government and rule the country directly. As the mobs marched, shots broke out between isolated groups of officers and the phalanxes of workers. Disorder quickly spread. There was some looting. Kerensky set out for the front immediately to find regiments to support the Provisional Government. But on that day and the tense night that followed, the demonstrations accomplished little besides arousing the population and letting off steam.

On the following day, July seventeenth, about six thousand sailors from the naval base at Kronstadt, just a few miles from Petrograd, arrived in destroyers to add their weight to the revolutionary movement. Kronstadt had long since been openly Bolshevik, and its sailors were always to be found in the forefront of every extreme action. Landing from their boats on the banks of the Neva, they made it their business to seize the Peter and Paul fortress, where they prepared to resist a siege. Meantime, the crowds, the Red Guards, the regiments were once again marching on the Tauride Palace. To groups who stopped before Bolshevik headquarters, Lenin spoke from the balcony. He advised them against any extreme action but applauded their spirit. But when the demonstrators reached the central districts of the city at midday, they came into sharp conflict with several small Cossack patrols who supported the Provisional Government. A pitched battle in which scores were killed and wounded took place between Cossacks and workers near the Liteiny Bridge. But under a hurricane of bullets from the crowd the Cossacks were forced to retreat in disorder.

By the time the demonstrators reached the Tauride Palace, they were in an ugly mood. Blood had been shed, men killed. What had their leaders in the Soviet to say to that? Why did the Soviet leadership refuse to take the power which the mob wanted to force upon it? All the carefully phrased, legalistic explanations offered by Menshevik orators could not explain that simple problem to the people.

As the huge demonstration descended on the Tauride Palace, Victor Chernov, the Menshevik leader and a minister in the Provisional Government, came out to speak. He referred scornfully to the Cadets and liberals who had withdrawn from the government but attempted to evade the question of taking power. Milyukov relates that a husky worker shook his fist under Chernov's nose and cried; "Take the power you ——, when they give it to you!" Even if apocryphal, the tale sums up the purpose and feeling of the crowd. Chernov would probably have been lynched then and there had not Trotsky rushed out and talked the crowd into letting him go.

In the evening those who supported the Provisional Government rejoiced to see a field regiment in full battle array marching down the Nevski Prospect toward the Tauride Palace. No doubt these were the forces sent by Kerensky from the front to suppress the demonstrations! In fact, the regiment was the 176th and it had come not to suppress the demonstration but to join it in suppressing the Provisional Government. When the regiment arrived at the Tauride Palace, it was met by the Menshevik leader Dan, dressed in a military uniform, who persuaded the men that they were meant to protect the palace against mobs. Thus the revolutionary regiment posted sentries to protect the very government it had set out to overthrow. Sukhanov, with considerable justification, points out this

141

incident as symptomatic of the confusion and purpose-lessness of the entire rising.

Finally two days and nights of armed demonstration, bloody street skirmishes, and endless argument convinced the workers and the regiments that they could not win their demands in this disorganized way. By dawn on July nineteenth the city was quiet. The sailors in the Peter and Paul fortress surrendered to the representatives of the Soviet and returned to Kronstadt. With the arrival in the city of a few regiments from the front, order was restored, and the July Days had ended.

But the Soviet leadership had suffered a bad fright. It seemed to them that most of the workers would listen only to Bolshevik leaders. The middle classes, who now made haste to flee the city, had also received a rude shock. It was apparent that to the masses of the people the revolution was not at an end. The situation contained all the seeds of civil war. When, on top of this, the Russian armies were being routed at the front, it was obvious that something direct and drastic would have to be done about the Bolsheviks. And for this the Provisional Government and the Soviet were ready.

On July seventeenth the government announced that it had conclusive evidence to prove that Lenin, Trotsky, and other Bolshevik leaders were paid agents of Germany. It released documents to the press to support this claim. It was made to appear that the demonstrations had been arranged by Lenin on instructions from the German high command to coincide with the German offensive at the front. The effect of the publication of these documents was stunning. Immediately it all seemed very clear—not only to middle-class liberals but also to workers and soldiers—that they had been betrayed—used by the Bolsheviks as pawns of German war policy. To get things started the government sent a gang of officers to wreck the offices and printing plant of *Pravda,* the Bolshevik newspaper. Another group rushed to Bolshevik headquarters to arrest the leadership. But they arrived too late. Lenin, with his sure and certain instincts of political survival, had already left Petrograd. He made his escape with Zinoviev to a forest outside the city, slept in a haystack for a few hours and then, disguised as a fireman on a train, crossed the border into Finland, where he went into hiding.

Other Bolsheviks, including Trotsky, stayed behind to face the music. A trial was organized under the auspices of the Menshevik and Social Revolutionary leadership of the Soviet. Despite a brilliant defense, Trotsky and the others were imprisoned in the Kresty Prison. But of greater importance was the complete wrecking of the Bolshevik organization, the bitter despair with which its supporters deserted by the thousands throughout Russia. Everywhere Bolshevik agitators had to go into hiding. The wrath of the workers, the peasants, and the soldiers howled about them like a violent thunderstorm.

How to explain this sudden revulsion on the part of the masses toward the Bolsheviks? First of all, the workers and soldiers were exhausted. For four months they had engaged in unremitting revolutionary activity. And to what result? Nothing had changed essentially. Hours were still long, pay low, food scarce—and the war continued. They were, for the moment, discouraged. Besides, they had just stubbed their toe against the government during the July Days and were resentful. A scapegoat was needed, and the government offered up the Bolsheviks. In the welter of confusion, fighting, and despair simple people turned to the simplest explanation—the idea of German agents disguised as Bolsheviks.

The government's evidence against the Bolsheviks

on this point has been debated again and again over the years. The documents involved do not stand up to careful examination, and many of the witnesses were former czarist police agents. Nevertheless there was an element of truth to the charges. Certainly the German high command did contribute money to the Bolshevik party—German records testify to that. And the Bolshevik insistence that the war be ended fitted in very well with German desires. On the other hand, American agents were unofficially advancing large sums of money to the Menshevik party during those months. And the Menshevik insistence that the war continue fitted in very well with American needs. In neither case was Bolshevik or Menshevik policy dictated by either Germany or the United States.

There is an element reminiscent of the postwar jitters that swept the United States in 1920 and again in 1948 about this whole affair. Under intense pressure, after an exhausting struggle, people seemed to grow hysterical regarding German agents, spies, saboteurs in Russia in 1917. Feeding this hysteria, the Provisional Government and the Soviet used it to break the Bolshevik power.

In defending himself against accusations of being a German spy, Trotsky declared: "A suspicion against us in that direction could be expressed only by those who do not know what a revolutionist is." And this strikes directly at the heart of the matter. The attempt —and there have been many over the years, right down to the present time—to explain the activities of Lenin and his followers in terms of German gold is not only irrelevant. It can be deluding in that it may blind people to actual historical dangers. The challenge posed by Bolshevism to capitalist society is much too serious to be dismissed or obscured by simpleminded charges of "espionage" or "treason."

In July and early August of 1917, however, the Bolshevik party reached its lowest point. A new government, with Kerensky as Prime Minister, was formed, and the liberal, middle-class, and conservative forces in Petrograd felt themselves strong enough to institute such measures as reimposing the death penalty in the army and tightening restrictions on public meetings and the press. True, Kerensky ruled mainly through default—no one else was willing to take on the job. But he enjoyed the support of the Allied ambassadors, of the middle classes generally, and of the moderate socialist leadership of the Soviet. That he could not continue long in office was clear to everyone. But who would replace him? The masses, haltingly led by the Bolsheviks in July, had attempted to seize power by forcing it into the unwilling hands of the Soviet. That attempt had failed, and the Bolsheviks were scattered, their power seemingly broken. Now, it seemed, was a favorable time for a blow from the right. For if the Soviet refused power, and Kerensky was too weak to hold it, and the Bolsheviks were in prison, there remained one group willing to take over the government: the former czarist autocracy and the former czarist generals. The forces of counterrevolution, which behind the confused facade of political upheaval had been biding their time, were now ready to strike.

CHAPTER SEVEN

The Counterrevolution

IN THE DEMORALIZATION of the workers, the scattering of the Bolsheviks, and the fright of the liberals which resulted from the July Days all those forces and opinions which had gone into hiding after the February Revolution saw what they imagined to be the dawn of new hope. The many thousands of old government officials who still served the Provisional Government much as they had served the Czar, the large landowners and industrialists, the rightist fanatics, and above all the officers and generals now thought they smelled an opportunity. Kerensky and his new government, they knew, represented no one and nothing. The Soviet, under the domination of rightist socialists, had proved itself easily led by the nose. The workers and the Bolsheviks were still disorganized from their July defeat. Here was an opportunity, and, as always in history, the opportunity produced a man to take advantage of it.

Lavr Georgievich Kornilov liked to refer to himself as a simple peasant. He had been born the son of a Siberian Cossack, and his slanting, Mongolian eyes and dark complexion spoke of an Oriental heritage. He was about the same age as Lenin—the only similarity between the two. Kornilov had made the army his life. Personally very brave and surprisingly energetic for a czarist general, he had made a good record on the Austrian front, where Russian troops had won their greatest victories. Captured early in the war, he made good his escape just before the February Revolution and displayed some resolution during the disaster of the Kerensky offensive. In reward for this, Kerensky promoted him to the post of Commander-in-Chief of all the Russian armies.

When Kornilov accepted his new appointment, he did so only after Kerensky had publicly assured him that the death penalty would be reintroduced in the army, the soldiers' committees abolished or bypassed, and strict controls established in the rear areas over railways and supply. He was a simple man—even his warmest supporters thought him simpleminded. General Alexeiev, the old czarist warhorse, described him as "a man with a lion's heart and the brains of a sheep." His political opinions were nonexistent; his solutions to such problems were the solutions of the barracks, the guardhouse. In the history of revolutions his figure is a familiar one—the strong man on horseback who is determined above all to establish "order" at any cost. His role had been filled in the past by such as Julius Caesar and Napoleon, in our own day by General Franco. But where his illustrious predecessors had possessed remarkable intelligence and acted within a historical situation which provided them with important support, Kornilov was empty-headed and acted in a vacuum.

It is perhaps a clear indication of the hopelessness and light-mindedness of the Russian liberal and conservative groups that they saw in Kornilov their only hope of salvation. Mikhail Rodzianko, the aging former president of the czarist Duma, sent him a telegram which read: IN THIS THREATENING HOUR ALL THINKING RUSSIA LOOKS TO YOU WITH FAITH AND HOPE. The Allied ambassadors (with the honorable exception of the American) saw in him their real hope of keeping Russia in the war. Besides that, various Cossack generals hastened to give him their support. There were almost four million Cossacks in Russia and, forgetting what had occurred on the streets of Petrograd in the first revolution, their leaders assumed them to be reliable supporters of reaction. Besides that there were thousands of disgruntled officers, there were the members of various military academies, there were such crack outfits as the Savage Division (troops of Caucasian tribesmen) and Kornilov's own personal bodyguard, uniformed in long red robes. On paper this seemed a formidable force to oppose the revolutionary regiments of Petrograd.

These regiments were now being purposely weakened by Kerensky. Every week hundreds and then thousands of the men were transferred to the front on one pretext or another. It was hoped in this way to undermine their revolutionary zeal. Actually, this short-sighted policy only poured thousands of confirmed revolutionaries into the front lines, where, as Trotsky observed, "they were to do a great work in the autumn." And the replacements which followed them into Petrograd were soon infected with revolutionary fervor. It was a sort of rotation system designed to produce revolutionaries.

But if Kerensky's policies seem stupid to the point of being suicidal, he had very little choice. His new government existed only as an uneasy compromise between the Soviet and the liberal and conservative forces. He felt himself obliged to play one against the other in order to maintain himself in power. Thus he threatened the Soviet with Kornilov and he threatened Kornilov with the masses. But the Soviet knew that Kerensky could have little control over Kornilov, and Kornilov knew that Kerensky had no influence with the masses.

The February Revolution had done away with the czarist autocracy, but it had not resolved the most important social questions. And now Russia was threatened by civil war between the possessing classes and the broad mass of workers and peasants. In this situation Kerensky was a living link between classes—and he constantly warned one side and then the other that his downfall would lead to civil war. In a desperate bid to round up some sort of support for his government, Kerensky called a State Conference of all classes and institutions to meet in Moscow on August twenty-fifth. Moscow was chosen because it was thought to be less revolutionary than Petrograd, and the State Conference itself was carefully designed to show that landlords, industrialists, church leaders, and officers commanded as much of a following among the masses as the socialist leaders. Delegates from factories employing thousands of workers found themselves seated alongside delegates from officers' clubs representing a handful. Yet every institution in Russia was represented. There were delegates from the four czarist Dumas, from various national groups such as the Ukrainians, from the Orthodox Church, from all the trades unions, from the peasantry, from the landlords, from the industrialists, the army, the navy—from every group or organization in Russia that could boast a desk or a letterhead. Only one group was not represented—the Bolsheviks, who had already denounced the conference as a sham.

The hatred of the Bolsheviks which had raged so strongly in mid-July had all but vanished by mid-August. The Provisional Government's denunciations of Lenin and Trotsky and the others had gone too far. The destruction of the Bolshevik newspaper *Pravda,* the closing down of Bolshevik headquarters, the arrest of the leaders, the driving of the party underground—all these measures had been too extreme. Within two weeks people—even Mensheviks and Social Revolutionaries—were feeling slightly guilty about it all. And the fantastic nature of the accusations—that Lenin was a German agent, and so on—only made them that much easier to refute. Besides, the Bolsheviks remained the only party demanding an immediate end to the war and immediate social reform. The workers, peasants, and soldiers really had no other party to turn to. Nor was it difficult for them to see that the most anti-Bolshevik people were the old czarist elements who meant to wreck their revolution. By joining with the most reactionary elements in Russia to destroy the Bolsheviks, the liberals and moderate socialists merely compromised themselves even further in the eyes of the masses. And when they bounced back, the Bolsheviks bounced back with a bang. Under the persecution the weak members of the party had drifted away. Those remaining were hard-core, totally dedicated members. By mid-August the membership rolls of the Bolsheviks had doubled, in spite of their illegal status.

Striving to create an illusion of solidarity, goodwill, and elevated moral tone, the State Conference was reminded of reality by a lightning strike of the workers of Moscow on the day it met. Streetcars did not run, newspapers were not printed, food was not delivered, industry was at a standstill, the shops were all closed. But the delegates resolutely ignored these manifestations of nonsupport as they opened their deliberations.

"The brilliant auditorium," Sukhanov recalled, "was quite sharply divided into two halves: to the right sat the bourgeoisie, to the left the democracy. In the orchestra and loges to the right many uniforms of generals were to be seen, and to the left ensigns and soldiers. Opposite the stage in the former Imperial Loge were seated the higher diplomatic representatives of the Allied and friendly powers . . . the extreme left occupied a small corner of the orchestra," the extreme left, in the absence of the Bolsheviks, being represented by independents.

Kerensky's opening speech was slightly hysterical, frightened. Speaking to the Conference from the stage, Kerensky declared that any new attempts against the government would be "put down with blood and iron." At this there was stormy applause from both right and left. "Whatever ultimatums, no matter who may present them to me," Kerensky cried, "I will know how to subdue him to the will of the supreme power, and to me, its supreme head." At this thinly veiled threat to Kornilovists, the left applauded, while the right maintained a glum silence. Winding himself up in histrionics, Kerensky shouted: "Do you not feel it in you, this mighty flame? . . . Do you not feel within you the strength and the will to discipline, self-sacrifice and labor? . . .

Do you not offer here a spectacle of the united strength of the nation?"

The liberal politician Paul Milyukov later wrote: "Many provincials saw Kerensky in this hall for the first time, and they went out half disappointed and half indignant. Before them had stood a young man with a tortured, pale face, and a pose like an actor speaking his lines. . . . In reality he evoked only a feeling of pity."

On August twenty-fifth General Kornilov arrived in Moscow. He had been invited to address the State Conference, although advised by Kerensky to limit himself to a brief outline of the military situation. But if anyone had any illusions about Kornilov's intentions, they were enlightened by the manner of his arrival. Trotsky described it acidly: "The Tekintsi [Kornilov's bodyguards] leaped from the approaching train in their bright red long coats, with their naked curved swords, and drew up in two files on the platform. Ecstatic ladies sprinkled the hero with flowers as he reviewed this bodyguard and the deputations. The Cadet Rodichev concluded his speech of greeting with the cry: 'Save Russia, and a grateful people will reward you!' Patriotic sobbings were heard. Morozova, a millionaire merchant's wife, went down on her knees. Officers carried Kornilov out to the people on their shoulders." Later Kornilov made his way with his entourage to the Ivarsky Church, where, in former days, the czars of Russia had prayed before their coronation.

And, in fact, Kornilov had already made certain preparations to seize power. He had deployed four cavalry divisions near Petrograd with the idea of using them to seize the city at the right moment. Kerensky, already growing suspicious that Kornilov wanted supreme power for himself (instead of winning it for Kerensky), had taken certain measures to "freeze" these divisions in their present encampments. But, with a much more serious intent and with no reference at all to Kerensky, the Petrograd and Moscow soviets had organized committees of defense. All during the State Conference, all during the speeches and the grand arrival of Kornilov the city of Moscow was effectively in the power of a soviet-appointed committee of two Mensheviks, two Social Revolutionaries, and two Bolsheviks! They had organized and prepared the Red Guards and the workers and revolutionary regiments against any attempt to seize power during the State Conference. The fact that two Bolsheviks shared equally in the direction of this committee is a good indication of both their resurgent power (they were still supposedly illegal) and of the recognition even by their enemies that only they could ensure the support of vast masses of the city workers.

On August twenty-seventh Kornilov made his speech to the State Conference. When he walked up to the platform, Milyukov recalled, "the short, stumpy but strong figure of a man with Kalmuck features appeared upon the stage, darting sharp piercing glances from his small black eyes in which there was a vicious glint. The hall rocked with applause. All leaped to their feet with the exception of . . . the soldiers." This was ominous; evidently the general was detested by just those men who knew him best, those he hoped to use to throttle the revolution.

Kornilov's speech was not inspired. After demanding the usual stern measures to restore discipline at the front, however, he exploded something of a bombshell in the crowded auditorium. "The enemy is already knocking at the gates of Riga," he declared, "and if the instability of our army does not make it possible to restrain him on the shores of the Gulf of Riga, then the road to Petrograd is open." The left-wing delegates understood by these words that Kornilov and his supporters would not hesitate to throw Petrograd to the Germans if that should prove necessary to destroy the revolution.

Right-wing and left-wing speakers now alternated
interminably on the platform. They insulted one another to the cheers and catcalls of supporters and enemies. The State Conference, intended as a demonstration of Russian unity, quickly developed into a miniature battlefield of coming civil war. The unreality of its
proceedings was climaxed finally by another of Kerensky's hysterical tirades. Milyukov described the
speech: "With a broken voice which fell from a hysterical shriek to a tragic whisper, Kerensky threatened an
imaginary enemy, intently searching for him throughout the hall with inflamed eyes. . . . 'Today, citizens
of the Russian land, I will no longer dream. . . . May
my heart become a stone. . . . Let all those flowers
and dreams of humanity dry up!' (A woman's voice
from the gallery: 'You cannot do that. Your heart will
not permit you.') 'I throw far away the key of my
heart, beloved people. I will think only of the state!' "
Kerensky's audience forgot their mutual hatreds as
they sat stupefied by this melodramatic speech. A feeling of complete bankruptcy, of hopeless despair hung
over the entire assembly. The State Conference in
Moscow was at an end.

The political maneuvering which now took place between Kornilov and Kerensky had about it elements of
farce. While Kerensky threatened and postured and issued orders to nonexistent forces Kornilov schemed
and deployed nonexistent armies against Petrograd.
Kerensky hoped to use Kornilov to destroy the Soviet
and then seize power for himself. Kornilov, on the
other hand, intended to destroy Kerensky and his Provisional Government just as soon as he had finished

with the Soviet, and proclaim himself dictator. Neither, of course, trusted the other.

Kornilov's basic plan was to use the officers' clubs and organizations in Petrograd to provoke a demonstration on the part of the workers. Then, on the excuse of putting down disorders in the capital, he would occupy the city with his own troops. He was to strike "not later than September fourteenth." Early in September telegrams flew between Kornilov and Kerensky. Kornilov invited Kerensky to come to army headquarters at Mogilev, where he would be "safe." Kerensky invited Kornilov to reveal all his plans in "fullest confidence." And in the theatrical manner of which he was as much the victim as the master Kerensky set fantastic traps for Kornilov and marched around the Winter Palace all night singing snatches of Italian grand opera to himself.

On September ninth the melodrama reached a crisis. On that day Kerensky, now really alarmed, ordered Kornilov to hand over command of the army to General Lukomsky and report immediately to Petrograd. Kornilov replied by assuming the order to have been issued under duress and ordering his men to advance on the capital. The tension built up by these two isolated men had risen out of all proportion to the power either could really command. But now a third force suddenly intervened.

The Petrograd Soviet had been watching the maneuvers of Kerensky and Kornilov with growing suspicion and alarm. Even though they continued to support Kerensky, the conservative socialists in the Soviet could not fail to recognize that his lunacy was putting their own heads into a noose. They secretly organized a Military Committee for the defense of Petrograd in which the Bolsheviks were heavily represented. Thus while Bolshevik leaders remained in prison and Lenin himself was in exile in Finland, their followers in Petrograd were issued arms and ammunition from government arsenals by the Soviet.

As if by magic, once again the revolutionary enthusiasm of the workers and soldiers in Petrograd soared high. Forty thousand Red Guards reported ready for action. Factories worked continuously to provide arms and cannons for the workers' militia; tens of thousands of men, women, and children appeared on the streets to dig trenches and erect barricades; the regiments in Petrograd prepared themselves for action; thousands of sailors came down from Kronstadt to report for duty; the trades unions armed and dispatched delegates to outlying districts to raise the alarm in the countryside around Petrograd. Overnight, it seemed, Petrograd had converted itself from a "chaotic mess" to a well-disciplined and grimly determined fortress.

But in the end there was to be no fighting. Kornilov was to be defeated by the revolution before he set foot in Petrograd—in fact, before his regiments even marched. Once again the railroad workers tore up tracks, diverted trains, and completely isolated Kornilov's divisions. Messages and telegrams were stopped at the telegraph office and handed over to Soviet representatives. As Trotsky observed, "The conspiracy was conducted by those circles who were not accustomed to know how to do anything without the lower ranks . . . without orderlies, servants, cooks, clerks, chauffeurs, messengers, laundresses, switchmen, telegraphers. . . . But all these little human bolts and links, unnoticeable, innumerable, necessary, were for the Soviet and against Kornilov. The revolution was omnipresent. It penetrated everywhere, coiling itself around the conspiracy."

One of Kornilov's crack regiments was composed of Caucasian mountaineers. Appropriately named the

Savage Division, it was said of them (by officers) that they didn't care who they slaughtered. It was this division which was to lead the way into Petrograd, but the railwaymen had effectively blocked its passage. And now while it waited a few miles outside the capital, agitators and delegates were sent out to it by the Soviet. The delegation was composed of Caucasian tribal chiefs; when it approached, the men of the Savage Division would not permit their officers to arrest it. Instead they listened to the delegates and then hoisted a red banner on the nearest staff car, arrested most of their officers, and declared against Kornilov.

Other regiments were subjected to this same method of infiltration, argument, explanation by delegations from the workers of Petrograd. In practically every case the regiments came over to the Soviet side. And those battalions who retained some loyalty to Kornilov found themselves lost on the railroad. Trains would move in the wrong direction, supplies would be sent to the wrong stations, artillery would disappear down the lengths of track, officer staffs would find themselves out of touch with their men; the humble railroad pawns were at work again—this time crying "Check!" to Kornilov. And while the railroad men stalled the troops the workers' delegates worked among them unceasingly. "Almost everywhere," General Krasnov wrote ruefully, "we saw one and the same picture. On the tracks or in the cars, or in the saddles of their black or bay horses . . . dragoons would be sitting or standing, and in the midst of them some lively personality in a soldier's long coat." That "lively personality" was the revolution's secret weapon—the soldier or worker or peasant who could explain things to his fellows. Against his obvious sincerity, the simplicity of his speech, his deeply personal understanding of the men with whom he talked—men like himself—all the schemes and plots, all the vainglorious proclamations of generals and politicians were pitiably inadequate. This agitator in his "soldier's long coat" was someone the soldiers could understand, and he said things they wanted to hear.

While Kornilov's forces thus melted away outside Petrograd, what of the two thousand officers within the city who were supposed to undertake such assignments as arresting all members of the Provisional Government and the Soviet, murdering selected socialist leaders, seizing control of communications centers? They simply disappeared. Many were drunk most of the time, some absconded with the money Kornilov had supplied for this venture, most were simply too frightened by events to leave their houses.

Meantime, throughout Russia the people were demonstrating against Kornilov. Moscow, Kiev, and other cities witnessed giant demonstrations against the General. The armies at the front barraged Petrograd with messages of support against him. The soldiers of the southern front arrested their general, Anton Denikin (who had been in on the conspiracy), while even Alexei Kaledin, leader of the Cossacks and a warm supporter of Kornilov, found it wiser to do nothing at all after he sounded out opinion among the Cossack rank and file.

On September twelfth General Krymov, commander of the Third Cavalry Corps and one of Kornilov's chief supporters, was arrested by his own men and sent to Petrograd a prisoner. There, after an interview with Kerensky, Krymov shot himself. The next day Kornilov himself was arrested and imprisoned in a monastery near Bikhov. The attempt at counterrevolution thus ended ignominiously, defeated not by Kerensky, who had prepared the ground for it, but by the workers and soldiers of Petrograd organized and led by the

Military Committee of the Soviet. If Kornilov had been revealed as an isolated and hopelessly deluded man, Kerensky had been shown to be equally isolated and equally incompetent. It seemed certain that the Provisional Government must now fall.

But fall it did not. Instead Kerensky made himself Commander-in-Chief of the army as well as Prime Minister, and appointed a small cabinet of five members (Kerensky, two moderate socialists, two army officers who were thought to have liberal leanings) which was soon dubbed "the Directory" after the counterrevolutionary body in France in 1795, which had executed Babeuf. Enjoying only the appearance of real power, Kerensky continued to rule on the sufferance of the Soviet—and the Bolsheviks.

The Kornilov revolt gave a powerful impulse to Bolshevism throughout Russia. It seemed clear to the masses now that their real enemies were not the slandered Bolsheviks but the czarist and liberal slanderers who had attempted to make war on them. More and more Bolshevik deputies were elected to the various committees and soviets across the country. And even within the conservative socialist parties dramatic changes took place. The Mensheviks, losing their grip on the workers, retained hold of the small shopkeepers, the government employees, certain army units, skilled craftsmen. But the Menshevik party was now split wide open on the war question. A group of Mensheviks who called themselves Menshevik-Internationalists and who followed most of the Leninist line was now disputing the leadership of the party with the "defensist" group. The Social Revolutionaries were likewise splitting. The new group within that radical peasant party called themselves Left Social Revolutionaries and sided with the Bolsheviks on all important questions. They claimed to represent the broadest layers of poor peasants, while the old Social Revolutionaries represented the richer peasants, all of which indicated a decided swing to the left among the people.

A new feeling of confidence swept through the workers, the Red Guards, the soldiers of the regiments. Had they not defeated Kornilov without firing a shot? A soldier of the armored car division, Mitrevitch, recalled: "There were nothing but stories of bravery and of great deeds and of how—well, if there is such bravery, we can fight the whole world. Here the Bolsheviks came into their own."

It was in elections to the various local Soviets, however, that Bolshevik strength was to prove most effective. During the July Days and after, while the rightist groups prepared the Kornilov adventure, they had succeeded in damaging not only the Bolsheviks but the Soviets as well. Symbolic of this was the way in which they forced the Petrograd Soviet to leave its meeting halls in the Tauride Palace and seek new quarters in the Smolny Institute, a former girls' school on the edge of the workers' districts of the city. In thus shoving the Soviet out, the rightists only pushed it deep into Bolshevik territory. At the end of September the Bolsheviks felt strong enough to demand new elections to the presidium (the governing board) of the Petrograd Soviet. The election meeting was one of unbearable tension, with the Soviet's hall in Smolny crowded with every delegate the various parties could round up. Everyone present knew that they were deciding the question of real power in Russia. True, there was the Provisional Government of Kerensky, and also the Executive Committee of the All-Russian Soviet—an august body of conservative socialists who had overall direction of Soviet policy—but all knew that neither of these groups could function without direct support from the Petrograd Soviet itself.

Trotsky, who, along with the other Bolshevik leaders, had been released from prison just a few days before, spoke sharply to the assembly. "When they propose to you to sanction the political line of the presidium, do not forget that you will be sanctioning the policies of Kerensky!"

Voting was by the usual device of having all deputies leave the hall who were in favor of overturning the old presidium and replacing it with Bolsheviks. As members drifted out of the hall, impassioned arguments broke out all over the Soviet. As more and more deputies left their seats the minutes passed with increasing tension. At last a count was taken. For the Bolsheviks 519; for the old presidium 414; abstaining 67. The Bolsheviks had won control of the central governing body of the revolution! Trotsky was immediately elected chairman of the Soviet presidium, with thirteen Bolsheviks, six Social Revolutionaries, and three Mensheviks on the presidium with him.

Trotsky recalled that the new presidium soon discovered that everything that could be taken away from the Soviet had already been removed by the former leadership: "The new leaders had nothing—no treasury, no newspapers, no secretarial apparatus, no means of locomotion, no pen and no pencil. Nothing but the blank walls and—the burning confidence of the workers and soldiers. That, however, proved sufficient."

And now, all over Russia, the Bolsheviks found themselves coming to power in the local soviets. The Moscow Soviet elected a Bolshevik chairman on September twenty-third, and the cities and provinces were following suit. The resolutions being passed under the new leadership were drastic: withdrawal of Soviet support for the Kerensky government, demands for land distribution—above all, demands for an early end to the war.

When he had arrived at the Finland Station months before to find himself isolated within his own party, Lenin had argued: "We are not charlatans. We must base ourselves only upon the consciousness of the masses. . . . Our line will prove right. All the oppressed will come to us. . . . They have no other way out." It had taken months of crisis and a counterrevolutionary attempt to justify this prediction, but at last it seemed to be coming true. And to Lenin, if not to all his followers, it was now apparent that the time had come for drastic and decisive action.

CHAPTER EIGHT

The Bolshevik Revolution

ON SEPTEMBER 25, 1917, Lenin, from his hiding place in Finland, wrote a letter to the Central Committee of the Bolshevik party in Petrograd. In it he declared that the Bolsheviks must organize immediately for an armed insurrection, a seizure of the state power. He went into detail—squads must be gotten ready to take over the telephone and telegraph buildings, the banks, the railroad stations; commissars must be appointed to direct the movements of the regiments; the entire General Staff must be arrested; the Kerensky government itself must be arrested. The time is ripe, Lenin declared; it would be criminal to wait any longer.

The Central Committee (the inner directorate of the Bolshevik party), in spite of the proclamations, speeches, and slogans, was aghast at these proposals. So terrified were its members by Lenin's demand that they actually burned his letters (copies were preserved). A second All-Russian Congress of Soviets had been called to meet in Petrograd on November second. With control of the Petrograd and Moscow soviets already in Bolshevik hands and soviets all over the country turning Bolshevik, it seemed to the Central Committee that they had only to wait for the congress and then maneuver it into declaring itself the government of Russia.

But Lenin, with his remarkable intuition for mass feeling, insisted that the Bolsheviks could not afford to wait. He raised the specter of another Kornilovist plot; he pointed to the flaming peasantry, the word-weary workers, and the war-weary army. Why couldn't the Central Committee see that all the power was now in its hands? It must prepare to seize power in Petrograd and Moscow and among the ships of the Baltic fleet. When the Central Committee still objected to his proposals, Lenin wrote a letter of resignation. He resigned from the Central Committee, he declared, in order to be free to propagandize his ideas among the lower echelons of the party. The resignation was never acted upon, but it illustrates the lengths to which Lenin was prepared to go to force the Bolsheviks into action. The arguments have much the same ring as the arguments of the preceding April, with Lenin standing almost alone and using the masses of ordinary Bolsheviks to force the hand of their more conservative leadership.

But there was a more precise and urgent reason for his attitude.

Russia was a land of peasants—well over 90 percent of the population. Without their support any revolution must fail; with their support any revolution would succeed. But the peasant is concerned above all else with the seizure of the land. Once that has been accomplished—that is, once the feudal regime of land ownership has been shattered and the land is divided among the peasantry—the peasant loses his revolutionary impulse. He becomes a landowner himself, with many of the interests of landownership. Thus, during the French Revolution the middle classes aroused the peasantry to seize the old feudal estates and kill the nobility. But once that had been done, the peasants in turn supported the middle classes in putting down the revolutionary attempts of the city workers.

Russia in 1917 lacked an energetic and determined middle class. History, as we have seen, passed them by, and when revolution came, they followed rather than led. Because of their weakness, the Russian middle classes were entirely too dependent upon the former aristocracy and the large landowners either to use or to prevent a peasant rebellion. After the February Revolution the conservative socialists and their allies, the liberals, had promised the peasantry that the land would be distributed—as soon as legal measures could be devised. But, like all other questions, the land question was continually postponed. All through the early months following the revolution the peasants waited patiently. As a liberal Moscow newspaper described them: "The muzhik [peasant] is glancing around, he is not doing anything yet, but look in his eyes—his eyes will tell you that all the land lying around him is his land." In April the Provisional Government received a telegram from one of the villages of Tambov province stating: "We desire to keep the peace in the interests of the freedom won. But for this reason, forbid the sale of the landlord's land. . . . Otherwise we will shed blood, but we will not let anyone else plow the land."

During the summer, as the Provisional Government hesitated and postponed, the peasants began to act. The government, having at its disposal no forces on which it could rely in the provinces, was helpless to interfere. By the beginning of September, Lenin warned: "Either . . . all the land to the peasants immediately . . . or the landlords and capitalists . . . will bring things to the point of an endlessly ferocious peasant revolt." This prediction proved accurate. A typical peasants' raid was described by Begishev, a peasant himself: "In September all rode out to raid Logvin. A troop of wagons and teams streamed out to his [Logvin's] estate and back, hundreds of muzhiks and wenches began to drive and carry off his cattle, grain, etc." A peasant from Tauride province named Gaponenko related: "The peasants began to raid the buildings, drive out the overseers, take the work animals, the machinery, the grain from the granaries. . . . They even tore off the blinds from the windows, the doors from the frames, the floors from the rooms, and the zinc roofs, and carried them away." Then, usually, the peasants put what remained to the torch. To those who objected that the burning of buildings which might one day be converted to schools and hospitals was senseless the peasants responded with the dearly bought wisdom of centuries of uprisings: We are burning the buildings so that the landlords will have no place to hide—if one destroys the wolves' nests, one must destroy the wolf, too.

By mid-September the Russian countryside was in flaming rebellion. The objectives of the peasants' uprisings had not changed, but more and more often they were following a Bolshevik lead. They were falling away from the Social Revolutionary party and the liberals as they saw that these groups would not help them seize the land. Referring to this fact, one peasant declared: "The Cadets never wore *armyaki* and *lapti* and therefore will never defend our interests." *Armyaki* were homemade woolen coats, *lapti* shoes of woven strips of tree bark. The fact that the Russian peasant was wearing bark for shoes in 1917 goes far to explain the intensity and ferocity of his struggle. It was this spirit of open rebellion that Lenin realized must be seized upon at once. To wait for the peasantry to get the land was to wait for them to become satisfied and even counterrevolutionary. This helps explain his sense of urgency.

While Lenin slowly won his argument with his own Central Committee the Kerensky government and those moderate socialists who still supported it in the Executive Committee of the All-Russian Soviet—a committee now stranded without backing, since the Bolsheviks had won control of the Petrograd Soviet itself—decided to call yet another conference of the conservative, liberal, and anti-Bolshevik socialist forces, this time in Petrograd. After much debate the conference elected members to a body to be known as the "Pre-Parliament"—an advisory body which would help rule Russia until the meeting of a Constituent Assembly. In so doing they hoped to bypass the now-Bolshevik-controlled soviets. All questions were to be postponed until the meeting of the Constituent Assembly, which would draft a parliamentary constitution for Russia. Lenin urged the Central Committee to ignore the Pre-Parliament—which, he maintained, was only a disguise for more postponement and plotting. But over his bitter objections the Bolsheviks sent a delegation of sixty, led by Trotsky, to the opening of the Pre-Parliament. But if Lenin was afraid this marked a weakening of Bolshevik determination, he need not have worried. After Kerensky made an opening speech, Trotsky was allowed ten minutes for "an emergency statement." While the more than five hundred delegates held their breaths, tension mounted feverishly. After condemning the Kerensky government as plotting to turn revolutionary Petrograd over to the Germans, and amid a storm of catcalls, insults, and rage, Trotsky concluded: "No, the Bolshevik faction announces that with this government of treason to the people . . . we have nothing whatever in common. . . . In withdrawing from the provisional council we summon the workers, soldiers, and peasants of all Russia to be on their guard and to be courageous. Petrograd is in danger! The revolution is in danger! The people are in danger! . . . We address ourselves to the people. All power to the soviets!" Having delivered this open declaration of war, the Bolsheviks walked out of the Pre-Parliament. Later, reporting on the walkout to the Petrograd Soviet, Trotsky cried: "Long live the direct and open struggle for a revolutionary power throughout the country!" These carefully chosen words meant exactly what they implied: Long live the armed insurrection!

The Bolsheviks, through the Petrograd Soviet, which had become an instrument of their policy, set up a Military Revolutionary Committee with Trotsky as its chairman. Representatives from all the trades unions, regiments, fleet units, Red Guards units were appointed to it. It was to be the instrument of insurrection, and although Lenin remained in overall authority, the actual uprising was to be led and inspired by Trotsky. Under the authority of the Military Revolutionary Committee was created a body known as the Permanent Conference of the Garrison—a uniting of the soldiers' committees of the various regiments in Petrograd for concerted action. Commissars were appointed for each regiment from the Military Revolutionary Committee.

On the surface, then, as the Bolsheviks prepared for a direct struggle for power, authority in Petrograd was divided among the Provisional Government of Kerensky, the conservative socialists of the All-Russian Executive Committee, and the Petrograd Soviet. The Pre-Parliament represented generally the interests of the Provisional Government and the conservative socialists, while the Military Revolutionary Committee represented the power of the Bolshevik-dominated Petrograd Soviet.

The question around which Trotsky decided to rally the uprising was that of whether to permit the Petrograd regiments to be sent away from the city by the General Staff.

September and early October had seen renewed German successes in the north. Riga had fallen and now Reval was threatened. The way to Petrograd seemed open. To Kerensky and the General Staff this seemed a golden opportunity to rid the city of its revolutionary regiments by sending them to the front to defend the city. Some transfers had been made and more were being ordered all the time. The Bolsheviks maintained that these maneuvers were part of a plot to destroy the Petrograd Soviet. In actuality there seems little doubt that there was an urgent necessity for troops to defend Petrograd at that moment, and the garrison regiments were obvious candidates for this task. After all, Petrograd was the capital of their revolution. That, at least, was Kerensky's attitude. But it is also true that many of the General Staff officers and the liberal and conservative groups saw in this necessity the opportunity of weakening the city's spirit. And in any event the workers and soldiers no longer trusted Kerensky any more than they did the General Staff—all had been tainted by well-founded suspicions of Kornilovism.

On the night of October twenty-third Lenin made his way into Petrograd in disguise. He wore a wig to cover his baldness and had shaved his beard. He had come to attend a secret meeting of the leading members of the Bolshevik Central Committee. For ten hours they debated whether or not the time was ripe for rebellion. Lenin hammered hard on the urgency of the project. He was opposed by Kamenev and Zinoviev but supported by Trotsky and most of the others. Stalin, as usual, did not commit himself until he saw how the majority would go. In the end Lenin won his point. A resolution was passed declaring that "an armed uprising has become inevitable and acute." From this night on, while Lenin returned to his hideout in Finland, the Bolsheviks took direct steps to raise a new revolution.

The first question was that of arming the workers. Although many had retained the weapons issued them by the Provisional Government when they defended the city against Kornilov, thousands had no rifles. Trotsky, chairman of the Military Revolutionary Committee, recalled in later years: "When a delegation from the workers came to me and said they needed weapons I answered: 'But the arsenals, you see, are not in our hands.' They answered: 'We have been to the Sestroretsk Arms Factory.' 'Well, and what about it?' They said that if the Soviet ordered they would deliver.' I gave them an order for five thousand rifles and they got them the same day. That was a first experiment." And one which was to be repeated successfully time and again in the coming days. The truth was simply that the factories and regiments had come more and more to recognize the Soviet as the only legitimate government. Therefore they accepted orders from it but not from Kerensky. More important than this, the Military Revolutionary Committee had already taken a poll among the Petrograd regiments and found that only one of them, the Ninth Cavalry, was against an uprising, while the Cavalry squadrons of certain Guards regiments would maintain neutrality.

In those days of feverish activity and speculation, it seemed that everyone in Petrograd was trying to figure out what the Bolshevik timetable would be. That an attempted rebellion would take place none doubted—only the date remained obscure. Most independent observers were convinced that the Bolshevik uprising would occur when the Second All-Russian Congress of Soviets met on November 7. What few seemed to understand was that a revolution was already in progress. Thus, for example, a delegation of workers would arrive from such-and-such an arsenal. The Military Revolutionary Committee would order them to issue weapons or to withhold them. And these orders were obeyed. But control of arsenals is one of the first prerogatives of a government. Likewise, the typographical workers' union approached the Committee to complain of an increase in the number of reactionary pamphlets. Henceforth the union agreed to print only those which met with the approval of the Committee. But this is a form of censorship—another function of a government. What was happening in bits and pieces was simply the transfer of actual power to the Soviet and its Military Revolutionary Committee away from Kerensky's government.

On Sunday, November fourth, the Petrograd Soviet called for mass meetings throughout the city. These were not to be street demonstrations but gatherings within the factories, meeting halls, and barracks—an informal review of the forces which would seize power. And the masses poured out in hundreds of thousands to hear the Bolshevik speakers, to swear undying loyalty to the Soviet, to listen and try to comprehend what was about to take place. Describing the huge crowds that crammed every possible meeting place in the city, Sukhanov—a non-Bolshevik—remarked that "there was a mood very near to ecstasy," while Trotsky recalled how "the experience of the revolution, the war, the heavy struggle of a whole bitter lifetime, rose from the deeps of memory in each of those poverty-driven men and women, expressing itself in simple and imperious thoughts: This way we can go no farther, we must break a road into the future." The same day the Military Revolutionary Committee warned the regiments that from now on they must obey only the commands of the commissars sent to them.

Kerensky, now at last thoroughly alarmed, called a special cabinet meeting for the evening of November fifth, and an emergency was declared to exist. The military governor of Petrograd, Colonel Polkovnikov, was placed in overall command of all forces in the city. The Military Revolutionary Committee was declared illegal, and the arrest of Trotsky and other Bolshevik leaders was ordered. Additional guards were posted outside the Winter Palace, where the Provisional Government met, and Cossack squadrons were ordered to the streets. But events had left Kerensky far behind. That same day the Military Revolutionary Committee had already dispatched telegrams to the various regiments ordering them to take up defensive positions in their areas with machine guns. The garrison of the Fortress of Peter and Paul, which at first refused to heed the commissar sent to them, were persuaded by Trotsky that afternoon to join the rebellion and turn over the arsenal to his committee.

In these last hours before the Bolshevik Revolution there were two Petrograds. The old, stately imperial city, which, in spite of the February Revolution, presented much the same appearance it had under the czars, showed until the last moment no signs of vanishing. True, there were little red flags stuck into the hands of the czarist monuments and long red streamers hanging down the fronts of the government buildings, but the palaces and ministries carried on their everyday work much as in years past. Militiamen with rifles slung over their shoulders had replaced the police on street corners, and the Czar and his family had been moved from Tsarskoe Selo to the Siberian province of Tobolsk (Rasputin's home province); but the army high command was still composed of czarist generals, and the members of the government bureaucracy still wore the uniforms appropriate to their rank—uniforms they had worn since the time of Peter the Great. Schoolboys still studied the same textbooks, and the children of the middle classes still told the old fairy tales about Ivan Czarevich. The ballet and opera carried on as before, and gay parties were still being held in restaurants and clubs.

The other Petrograd centered around the Bolshevik Soviet at Smolny Institute. John Reed, an American correspondent who later became a Communist, described this other Petrograd in his book *Ten Days That Shook the World*. Entering Smolny, he noted that the former classrooms for aristocratic young ladies were "white and bare, on their doors enameled plaques still informed the passer-by that within was 'Ladies Classroom Number 4,' or 'Teachers' Bureau'; but over these hung crudely lettered signs, evidence of the vitality of the new order, 'Central Committee of the Petrograd Soviet,' etc. The long, vaulted corridors, lit by rare electric lights, were thronged with hurrying shapes of soldiers and workmen, some bent under the weight of huge bundles of newspapers, proclamations, printed propaganda of all sorts. The sound of their heavy boots made a deep and incessant thunder on the wooden floor." Going downstairs, Reed bought a meal ticket for two rubles and joined a long line of workers, soldiers, and Red Guards in line as women ladled out cabbage soup and served chunks of meat. Outside, beneath a steady drizzle of rain, he saw hundreds of workers and soldiers rushing about on various missions, protective barricades being set up around Smolny itself, and machine guns being placed.

Early on the morning of November sixth government officials with a detachment of officers closed down the Bolshevik printing plant and sealed the doors. At once several of the workers ran over to Smolny, where they found Trotsky. If the Military Revolutionary Committee would give them a guard, they would bring out the paper. Immediately Trotsky ordered detachments of the Litovsky regiment to open the plant and protect the workers against the Provisional Government forces. Within hours the Bolshevik newspaper was back on the streets. The cruiser *Aurora*, packed with Bolshevik sailors, was at anchor in the Neva. The Provisional Government ordered it to sea. Instantly the sailors asked Smolny whether they should obey the order. Trotsky replied that they were to stay where they were and prepare for action—an order which was immediately obeyed. This was clearcut insurrection. And from the Fortress of Peter and Paul, wagonloads and truckloads of guns were being carried away—on Trotsky's orders—to arm the Red Guards, while within the fortress troops were cleaning and preparing their Colt machine guns.

Meanwhile Kerensky found time to make yet another speech to the delegates of the Pre-Parliament, meeting at the Mariinsky Palace. He read out one of the Military Revolutionary Committee's orders which had fallen into his hands. It was addressed to the Petrograd regiments and instructed: "Make the regiments ready for battle and await further orders." Now, Kerensky declared, he had proof positive that the Bolsheviks intended to rise. He would deal with them ruthlessly, and he asked for a vote of confidence from the meeting. He left the palace soon afterward—and never did receive his vote of confidence, as the delegates within fell to arguing and bickering among themselves.

That night the Bolsheviks struck. The city had already been divided into convenient districts. Within each district were posted patrols and squads from the garrison regiments, Red Guards detachments, and workers' committees. Each of the districts had a well-thought-out plan of operations for the seizure of the strategic buildings and services within the district. All night long the plan went forward: seizure of the railroad stations, the telephone exchange, the telegraph building, the state banks, the printing plants, the regimental barracks. A guard would be posted, and a commissar appointed by the Military Revolutionary Committee would take over the direction of operations in each institution. Where the workers were not already Bolshevik, sentries would be posted inside as well as outside the building. Nowhere was there any resistance; in most places the workers cheered when their buildings were occupied.

Meanwhile, the Second All-Russian Congress of Soviets were gathering at Smolny. For days the delegates had been arriving. The Bolsheviks intended to have already captured the power before the Congress opened, but their schedule was slightly faulty. At three thirty in the morning, while Bolshevik detachments were seizing control of Petrograd, a Menshevik who was present at

177

the Congress reported: "A meeting of the Central Executive Committee together with the delegates to the Congress of Soviets is in progress with an overwhelming majority of Bolsheviks. Trotsky has received an ovation. He has announced that he hopes for a bloodless victory of the insurrection, since the power is in their hands. The Bolsheviks have begun active operations. They have seized the Nikolaevsky Bridge and posted armored cars there. The Pavlovsky regiment has posted pickets on Milliony Street near the Winter Palace, is stopping everybody, arresting them, and sending them to Smolny Institute. . . . The Baltic railroad station is also in the hands of the Bolsheviks. If the front does not interfere, the government will be unable to resist. . . ."

At 10 A.M. on November seventh Trotsky issued a proclamation declaring that the Provisional Government had fallen and that all power had passed into the hands of the Soviet and its Military Revolutionary Committee. As Trotsky was later to admit, "In a certain sense this declaration was very premature. The government still existed, at least within the territory of the Winter Palace . . . the provinces had not yet expressed themselves . . . In order to get complete possession of the power it was necessary to act as a power."

At noon, squads of Red Guards and a few armored cars arrived at the Mariinsky Palace, where the Pre-Parliament was sitting. The delegates, in a state of acute alarm, were being told that all would be well— that Kerensky had gone off to the front to raise loyal regiments—when soldiers of the Litovsky regiment appeared in the hall. Their commander ordered the delegates to leave the building. After a hasty protest, the delegates dispersed, bringing the Pre-Parliament to an end after eighteen days of life. The news about Kerensky was correct, however. He had borrowed a car from the American Embassy and, over the Embassy's protests, driven off with the American flag on the fender as his protection. The ruse was successful, and he slipped out of the city.

Now all attention centered upon the Winter Palace. There, in the ornate Malachite Chamber, the ministers of Kerensky's government endlessly debated what they could or should do. The debate was meaningless, since they had no forces at their disposal other than a volunteer Women's Battalion and the young cadets of a few military academies who were posted on guard around the immense building. Their leader, Kerensky, had promised troops from the front—but would there be time? From their windows the ministers could see the cruiser *Aurora* landing detachments of sailors and, beyond, the guns of the Fortress of Peter and Paul pointed threateningly in their direction. By 6 P.M. the Winter Palace had been surrounded by Bolshevik detachments. Seven warships from the Baltic fleet had also arrived, crammed with revolutionary sailors. The Bolsheviks now sent an ultimatum to the ministers within: either surrender or we shall start shelling the palace. After a hasty discussion the ultimatum was rejected, and the ministers moved into a room deeper within the palace.

"We wandered," one of the ministers later recalled, "through the gigantic mousetrap, meeting occasionally, either all together or in small groups, for brief conversations—condemned people, lonely, abandoned by all. . . . Around us vacancy, within us vacancy, and in this grew up the soulless courage of placid indifference."

Two blank shots were fired—one from the *Aurora* and one from Peter and Paul, at 9 P.M. They were the signal for a not very effective, slow, and indifferently accurate shelling of the Winter Palace. A few windows were broken, a few stones sent flying. But the shelling decided the Women's Battalion to flee, with a few Cossacks and Cadets. Soon groups of Red Guards penetrated the huge building, wandering through its echoing corridors, where they occasionally ran into and captured officers and Cadets. John Reed was admitted into the building on the strength of his American passport and recalled that the porters on duty at the main entrance, still wearing their ornate uniforms, politely took his coat. Meantime the shelling continued slowly and without inflicting casualties.

Around midnight the Petrograd City Duma, which had been in session for hours amid the greatest confusion, decided that it must march to the Winter Palace and die by the side of the government ministers. After a series of rousing speeches, the handful of Duma delegates set out under the leadership of Burgomaster Schreider and one of the government ministers, Prokopovitch, who had somehow not yet joined his fellows inside the Winter Palace. Schreider and Prokopovitch carried lanterns and as the little procession marched through the empty streets of Petrograd they sang the "Marseillaise." At the Ekaterininsky Canal the procession was stopped by a patrol of armed sailors who advised them to go home. Someone in the procession called out that they should die on the spot. The sailors shrugged—if that was the way they wanted it. But Prokopovitch spoke to his followers, waving an umbrella, and persuaded them that to die under the sailors' guns would be to tempt the sailors into a grave sin. "Let us return to the Duma," he cried, "and talk over methods of saving the country and the revolution." The procession agreed and returned to the Duma—without singing.

By 1 A.M. on November eighth resistance within the

Winter Palace was crumbling. More and more Red Guards had infiltrated the building. Government officers rushed about disarming workers, and workers rushed about disarming officers. Soon only confusion reigned, but nobody was hurt. The workers and Red Guards swarmed over the parquet floors of the palace, rushed through the huge, tapestry-hung rooms, burst finally into the room in which sat the government ministers. At 2:10 A.M. on November eighth the Provisional Government was placed under arrest. Later its members were taken to the Fortress of Peter and Paul. With their arrest the Provisional Government, which had ruled Russia since the February Revolution, came to an end.

Meanwhile the Congress of Soviets continued its sessions at Smolny Institute amid an uproar. Mensheviks, Social Revolutionaries, and Independents denounced the action of the Bolsheviks—but the dissenters were in a very small minority. To a demand on the part of Martov's independent group that the Bolsheviks seek a compromise with the conservative socialists and the liberals (all of whom had already walked out on the Soviet Congress) Trotsky replied: "No, a compromise is no good here. To those who have gone out, and to all who make like proposals, we must say, 'You are pitiful isolated individuals; you are bankrupts; your role is played out. Go where you belong from now on —into the rubbish can of history!' "

And amid this uproar news was continually arriving. The Winter Palace had surrendered. The troops Kerensky had dispatched from the front had refused to march. The commanding general of the northern front had agreed to submit to the Congress. "Men weeping, men embracing," John Reed reported the elation with which these messages were received. After electing an overwhelmingly Bolshevik Central Committee, the Soviet Congress adjourned until the evening.

During the day (November eighth) the Bolsheviks decided to organize a new cabinet. It would be called the Soviet of People's Commissars and would consist only of Bolsheviks. Lenin, who had returned to Smolny only the day before, and who had been sleeping on the floor of one of the rooms, was to be head of the new government. At 9 P.M. the Soviet Congress reassembled to ratify these measures. Now at last Lenin appeared on the platform and was greeted by an immense ovation. John Reed reported: "Now Lenin, gripping the edges of the reading stand, let little winking eyes travel over the crowd as he stood there waiting, apparently oblivious to the long-rolling ovation, which lasted several minutes. When it finished, he said simply, 'We shall now proceed to construct the socialist order.' Again that overwhelming human roar."

Lenin proposed immediate peace—without indemnities, without annexations. The peace appeal would be directed to all governments—and also to the peoples behind those governments. Next he proposed that all private ownership of land in Russia be abolished. Nothing was to be paid to the landowners. Both proposals were adopted by the Congress. Later the new government appointments (including Lenin as President, Trotsky as Commissar for Foreign Affairs) were approved and the meeting adjourned.

The seizure of power by the Bolsheviks in Petrograd has been characterized by many historians as a mere "stroke" on the part of the Bolshevik leadership, not a revolution. The quiet and bloodless takeover of the machinery of government, the absence of mobs on the streets, the swiftness with which everything moved did seem to give that impression. But, in fact, the revolution had been going on for months. The ultimate seizure of power was only a minor operation. The very fact that the Bolsheviks required no mobs in the streets, no barricades and regiments—only the patrols sent out to accomplish their various tasks—spoke of tremendous power behind the scenes. Trotsky, the revolution's supreme commander, reflected many years later: "Only with heavy reserves behind them could revolutionary detachments go about their work with such confidence. The scattered government patrols, in contrast, being convinced in advance of their own isolation, renounced the very idea of resistance. The bourgeois classes had expected barricades, flaming conflagrations, looting, rivers of blood. In reality a silence reigned more terrible than all the thunders of the world. The social ground shifted noiselessly like a revolving stage, bringing forward the popular masses, carrying away to limbo the rulers of yesterday."

CHAPTER NINE

Triumph and Tragedy

IF THE BOLSHEVIK VICTORY in Petrograd had been almost bloodless, there was bitter fighting in Moscow. There the forces of the Provisional Government barricaded themselves within the mighty walls of the Kremlin and surrendered only after days of intensive shelling. Telegrams had gone out from Petrograd to cities and villages all over Russia announcing the overthrow of the Provisional government and the transfer of power to the Soviet. These telegrams sparked off local uprisings and, in some cases, bloody strife. Although the overwhelming majority of the provinces followed the Bolshevik lead, there were notable exceptions. Thus, in Kiev, ancient capital of the Ukraine, the people, seeing at last a chance to escape from Russian domination, began to form a separate government. The same independence movements were noticeable in certain areas of Siberia and the Caucasus. The position of the Cossacks was far from certain. And what of the many hundreds of thousands of German and Austrian prisoners of war, scattered all over Russia? In many areas they outnumbered the local population—and they were experienced soldiers. Now that central authority seemed to be tottering, they might seize the opportunity to rebel and escape. Besides, there was the problem of what the Allies would do now that a government committed to end Russian participation in the war had come to power.

In Petrograd itself things were far from clear. During the Bolshevik uprising and in the days immediately afterward high government officials had been arrested along with bankers, officers, and other upper-class leaders, but in most cases they had been released immediately. Now they, in combination with the outcast conservative socialist leaders, began to organize Committees for the Salvation of the Fatherland in Petrograd and throughout the country. And, taking their cue from their former employers, all the government clerks, the skilled telephone and telegraph technicians, the bank clerks, and the post office workers went on strike. Decrees issued by the new government could not be processed through the normal channels, messages could not be delivered, no money could be issued. Besides that, and more important, the railroad workers' union (dominated by conservative socialists) declared itself opposed to the Bolshevik takeover. As yet, in spite of the defection of the regiments Kerensky had ordered from the front, the front-line armies had not spoken. If those armies came out against the Bolsheviks, then nothing could save them. It was on this possibility that the Committees of Salvation and the clerks based their struggle.

Lenin's means of handling this sort of opposition was simply to refuse to recognize that it existed. He acted as if the Bolshevik government had, in fact, all the power to do that which it proclaimed. Decrees and laws now flooded out of Petrograd in a torrent. Nothing like it had been seen before. Private ownership of land was abolished; banks were nationalized; all industrial enterprises were nationalized; the merchant marine was nationalized; the stock market was simply abolished; the right of inheritance was abolished; gold was declared a state monopoly; all governmental debts were declared null and void. The old criminal courts were replaced by revolutionary tribunals in which any citizen could act as judge or lawyer; the old strict marriage and divorce laws were replaced by very lenient civil codes. The church was not abolished, but its lands were seized, and religious teaching was forbidden in the schools. The old Russian calendar was discarded in favor of the Western calendar, and the Russian alphabet was modernized. All the old titles of aristocracy and rank were swept away to be replaced by *Citizen* or, more commonly, *Comrade*. A law was passed which suppressed the conservative newspapers "temporarily."

Elections to a Constituent Assembly were set for November twenty-fifth. A note was sent to the governments of all the warring powers proposing an immediate armistice. But the Allies ignored this message and refused to recognize the new Bolshevik government.

On November eleventh a group of officers made an attempt to storm the Petrograd telephone exchange.

They succeeded in penetrating the building, and even in cutting Smolny's communications. But detachments of Red Guards forced them out after a day of heavy fighting. The question of what to do about the strike of government and bank employees was serious. If the Bolsheviks could easily seize buildings and replace workers, they could not train people overnight to carry on the complicated business of government. "All were against them," John Reed recalled, "—businessmen, speculators, investors, landowners, army officers, politicians, teachers, students, professional men, shopkeepers, clerks, agents. The other socialist parties hated the Bolsheviks with an implacable hatred. On the side of the Soviets were the rank and file of workers, the sailors, the undemoralized soldiers, the landless peasants, and a few—a very few—intellectuals."

Meantime, Trotsky had hurried off to the front to ascertain the feelings of the divisions and regiments on which the Committees of Salvation were basing their hopes. After a whirlwind tour, during which he tested the feelings of the troops, he was able to report: "The night of November 12th–13th will go down in history . . . Kerensky is retreating. We are advancing." In fact, those huge armies of landless peasants and revolutionary city workers expressed almost unanimous support for the Bolsheviks. Smolny was now able to issue an order: "To all army corps, divisional and regimental committees, to all soviets of workers, soldiers, and peasants' deputies, to all, all, all: we demand that Kerensky be arrested." This order, however, was too late. Disguised as a sailor, Kerensky had already slipped through the Bolshevik net. Later, with the help of a British secret agent, he made his way to London and finally to the United States.

On November twenty-fifth the countrywide elections to the Constituent Assembly took place. The idea of a

Constituent Assembly—an elected congress representing the wishes of all the people who would draft a democratic constitution for Russia—had been at the core of Russian revolutionary thought for centuries—not Bolshevik thought, to be sure, but the hopes and dreams of thousands of revolutionary martyrs had been centered upon it. Out of nearly forty-two million votes cast the Bolsheviks won about 30 percent, the Social Revolutionaries (representing the peasants) won about 58 percent, while the conservative and middle-class parties won only two million votes between them. It has been held by Trotsky and other of the Bolshevik leaders that this Assembly was in fact a counterrevolutionary body. This claim is largely based on the highly disputable fact that the Social Revolutionaries, who held an overwhelming majority of the delegates, did not truly represent the broad masses of the peasantry. And here the Bolsheviks were running up against the problem which was to plague Soviet governments for decades to come—the peasantry. There was no doubt that the peasantry was revolutionary at that moment; estates burning all over Russia testified to the fact. But the peasant, led by the Social Revolutionary party, was fighting for *ownership* of the land. The Bolsheviks intended to *nationalize* the land. During the early days this conflict was not apparent, and there is some truth to the Bolshevik contention that under the immediate circumstances they better represented the interests of the masses of poorest peasants than did the Social Revolutionaries. Nonetheless, it was the Social Revolutionaries who had been elected.

The Bolshevik answer to this electoral defeat was ruthless. When the Constituent Assembly gathered in Petrograd on January 18, 1918, the delegates and their crowds of supporters had to fight their way through ranks of Bolshevik soldiers and sailors to enter the Tauride Palace. Inside, the Bolsheviks carried on an uproar that made orderly proceedings all but impossible. At last Bolshevik troops forcibly ejected the delegates from the Palace and thus brought to an end all idea of formal democracy in Russia. Many of the delegates escaped abroad; others joined the gathering forces of those who opposed the Bolsheviks by force of arms.

The Bolshevik reaction to the Constituent Assembly brings us face to face with the central problems, both historic and psychological, of the Bolshevik power in Russia. If, as they claimed, the Bolsheviks enjoyed the support of the overwhelming mass of the people, why did they find it necessary to use the methods of czarism to disperse an assembly elected by those people? If, even though in a formal minority, "history" was to drive the peasants into their ranks very quickly, why did the Bolsheviks find it necessary to use rifles and bayonets to prod history along? The answers offered by the Bolsheviks—that in the midst of a gathering civil war there is no time for formal debate, that the Constituent Assembly was outdated even before it met, that it was to be used by a counterrevolutionary conspiracy, and so forth—do not ring true. Historical answers—for example, the fact that it was the French peasantry who undermined and finally destroyed the French Revolution—only serve to bring into question the entire Bolshevik conception of historical "inevitability." These are questions Márx and Engels did not evade. It was because of this very problem of peasantry that they had predicted the socialist revolution would have to begin in those countries in which industrialization had eliminated the peasantry. Events in Russia were to prove them correct—and no amount of Bolshevik wordage has ever been able to obscure this fact. Russia was a land of peasants. The peasants wanted only the land. The Social Revolutionaries represented them perfectly in this respect. The Bolsheviks, who enjoyed overwhelming support among the city workers and among the armies in which millions of peasants had been divorced from the land and organized under worker leadership, would have to short-circuit their own Marxist view of history to force socialism onto a nation which had not yet emerged into capitalism. This had been behind the struggle with the conservative socialists. It was a problem which was to prove insoluble—except at a fearful price, much later on. The Bolsheviks were prepared to pay this price. But this in turn brings into question the entire psychology of the Bolsheviks. That they fought courageously and nobly to bring to an end an intolerable regime no one would deny—so did many other groups in Russia. That they clearly saw the inconsistencies of their enemies and were swift to take advantage of them is also true. That under the circumstances they represented the interests of the city workers and soldiers seems indisputable. But in arguing and fighting against czarism, against the most reactionary type of semicapitalism, against the fraud represented by Kerensky and his followers, the Bolsheviks were tilting against straw dummies. Just as they themselves would have said, their true judge was "history." How, then, could a group of men who had devoted their lives to a struggle for freedom, who had loudly proclaimed their submission to "historical inevitability," find themselves compelled to abolish freedom and defy "history"? It has been said that all power corrupts, and absolute power corrupts absolutely. But the first indications of Bolshevik ruthlessness in command came long before they had won absolute power.

For many years the Bolsheviks had been forced to

operate underground in an atmosphere of conspiracy and violence. Most of the leaders of the party had become indifferent to violence, had slowly developed the psychology of the conspirator who sees enemies everywhere, who cannot afford to trust even his closest associates. Besides, they had for years held aloft in isolation the banner of the "one true faith." There is about them something of the psychology of the religious fanatic. With "history" elevated to the place of God, they can do no wrong—neither murder, the suppression of freedom, nor even the betrayal of "history" itself can be wrong to the possessors of the only truth. The closest historical parallel to the psychology of the Bolshevik leadership is in some respects that of the Holy Inquisition which plagued Europe centuries ago. The fact that such a psychology may have been forced upon them by events cannot excuse its fearful results.

Trotsky has suggested that Lenin, Kamenev, himself, and others of the Old Bolshevik leadership escaped this psychology. He has pointed out the relative freedom of debate within Bolshevik ruling circles during the early years, the high intelligence of some of the leaders, their humanity. He has blamed the subsequent horrors of dictatorship upon Stalin and others who had "betrayed" the revolution. But the inner contradictions, the external disasters, and the rigid terror of Bolshevik rule became apparent long before Lenin's death and Trotsky's exile. To explain them in terms of immediate struggle begs the question. Perhaps the fundamental truth from which the Bolsheviks could not and cannot escape is that any man or group of men who seek to define Man in their own rigid terms—no matter what those terms may be—and who then try to force him into the mold they have conceived are reduced at last to violence and terror as their chief weapons. This has been true throughout history and remains true today. Man is entirely too complicated, elusive, and sublimely chaotic a creature to fit anyone's preconceived patterns.

But in 1918, with world war raging, with the Bolsheviks preparing for a bitter civil war against the forces of counterrevolution, there was little time for such reflections. The Bolsheviks had come to power on the promise of immediate peace, and this promise they now proceeded to honor.

Trotsky had been in contact with the Germans regarding peace since the end of November 1917. Lenin and the Bolshevik leadership still hoped for a general, worldwide peace conference in which no indemnities or annexations would be demanded. But the Allies had no intention of entering such a conference. Instead they sent a note to General Dukhonin, who commanded the Russian armies, warning him against entering into any negotiations with the Germans. Caught between the Bolshevik demand for an immediate armistice and the Allied demand for continued fighting, with his armies going to pieces all around him, Dukhonin defied the Bolshevik order. The Petrograd Soviet immediately dispatched a naval ensign, Nikolai Krylenko, who had been active in the revolutionary movement in Kronstadt, to take over supreme command of the Russian armies. Krylenko arrived at headquarters on December third. The soldiers at once arrested Dukhonin and, in spite of Krylenko's attempts to save the old general, lynched him.

On the same day a Russian delegation arrived at the city of Brest-Litovsk to negotiate an armistice with the Germans. After brief discussion it was agreed that fighting should be suspended for two weeks to allow both sides time to prepare their peace terms.

To the Germans peace with Russia was now a necessity. American troops were pouring into western

Europe, and Germany could no longer wage war on two fronts. Besides, Germany suffered heavily from the British blockade and needed the raw materials and food which trade with a peaceful Russia might provide. They were disposed therefore to make a quick peace —but one which would insure them against any further attack from the east and give them control of the resources they needed. The Bolsheviks, on the other hand, hoped to draw out the negotiations as long as possible. They had great hopes for the revolutionary movements in Germany and Austria, and they also realized that it was only a matter of time before the Allies won on the Western Front. They issued numerous orders to Russian troops to fraternize with the Germans facing them, hoping to ignite a rebellion in the German army—and contact was made with German socialists who, it was hoped, would force the Kaiser to make a liberal peace.

With the Russians employing every possible delaying tactic, the negotiations dragged on for weeks. Trotsky at last went so far as to tell the Germans that the Russians would neither fight nor sign a peace treaty. In any event, the German General Staff brought things to a decision by the simple expedient of ordering their troops to advance. Against little opposition from the ruined Russian armies, German forces swept forward all along the front. At Kiev they signed a separate armistice agreement with the anti-Bolshevik Ukrainian government which had seized control. German patrols were now almost within sight of Petrograd. By March third the Russians could delay no longer. They signed a peace treaty with Germany at Brest-Litovsk.

By the Treaty of Brest-Litovsk, Russia lost about one third of her population to the Germans and one quarter of her territories, more than half of her industries, and a huge portion of the national income. It was one of the harshest peace treaties in history, and if it crushed Russia, it alerted the Western Allies to the necessity of fighting through to complete victory against the Kaiser.

With the collapse of Russia as an ally in the war against Germany, England, France, Japan, and the United States had now to consider what steps they could take to prevent Allied arms and equipment from falling into German hands. There were very large munitions dumps both at Archangel and at Vladivostok. But if the fate of these supply depots, with their hundreds of thousands of tons of war materiel, worried the Allied governments, this was not their only motive for intervening directly in Russian affairs.

The ruling circles in both France and England viewed with horror the Bolshevik rise to power. By intervening with supplies, money, and men, they hoped to encourage those who still fought the Bolsheviks. French and English policy looked toward the overthrowing of the Bolshevik regime. The Japanese were concerned solely with how much Russian Far-Eastern territory they could grab amid the chaos and how much of former Russian influence they could usurp. The Americans, on the other hand, were inclined not to interfere in Russian internal affairs. Woodrow Wilson resisted all British and French attempts to talk him into a new war against the Bolsheviks. American troops were to be included in the British expedition to Archangel and Murmansk, but solely to help protect the supply depots against the Germans. In the Far East, American troops were sent to Vladivostok on the same mission—but also to make certain that the Japanese did not use the occasion to seize Russian territory. When the Bolsheviks later accused Britain and France of helping prolong the agony of the civil war in an attempt to overthrow them, they were correct. The same accusation leveled against the Americans was completely incorrect.

The British and French attempts at intervention were doomed in advance to end in fiasco. In Archangel, in Vladivostok, in the Crimea, wherever they sought to fight against the Bolsheviks, they soon found that their only allies were just those generals and politicians who had been most hated by the Russian people. With no popular support in Russia, war-weariness at home, and the growing strength of the Bolshevik power, foreign intervention soon collapsed, but not before it had produced one of the most remarkable events in military history—the odyssey of the Czechoslovakian Legion.

The Czech Legion was originally composed of former Austrian-Czech soldiers who had been captured by the czarist armies and certain Russian-Czech elements. These men fought for the creation of an independent Czechoslovakia against the Germans and Austrians. When the Russian armies collapsed, they alone retained their morale and fighting discipline. The Russian Revolution had little interest for them—they wanted only to return to an independent and free Czechoslovakia. When the Germans seized control of most of the Ukraine after Brest-Litovsk, this corps, after fighting a heavy rearguard action to avoid encirclement, retreated in good order toward the Ural Mountains. They were very well armed and were under the direct orders of the Allied Supreme Command in Paris. With the Russian collapse it was proposed to evacuate the Czech Legion from Russia. But the only way to get out seemed to be through Vladivostok on the Pacific. Accordingly the Czech Legion commenced a three-thousand-mile march across Siberia to Vladivostok. They immediately ran into difficulties along the way with the local Soviet authorities, who suspected them of collaborating with counterrevolutionary forces. In May 1918 fighting broke out between the Czechs and the Bolsheviks along the line of their retreat. The Czechs immediately seized control of the Trans-Siberian Railroad and leagued together with all the anti-Bolshevik Russians in the three-thousand-mile corridor along the railroad. Soon the forty thousand men of the Czech Legion found themselves strung out in enemy territory from the Ural Mountains to Vladivostok guarding the line of the Trans-Siberian. It was in order to help the Czechs escape through Vladivostok that American troops were originally dispatched to that city.

One unexpected result of the Czech Legion's uprising was the murder of ex-Czar Nicholas II and his family. In April 1918 the Romanov family had been taken to Ekaterinburg in the Urals, where they were imprisoned in a local merchants's house. They were jealously guarded by the extremely hostile local soviet. In July a rumor swept through the little village: the Czech Legion was approaching, and with it various czarist and counterrevolutionary forces! If they liberated Nicholas or his family, would they not try to rally forces around him to regain the throne? The Russian Revolution at this moment had reached that same problem faced by the English Revolution of the seventeenth century and the French Revolution of the eighteenth: what to do with the deposed ruler who may become a threat to the revolution. They answered it the same way. On July sixteenth Nicholas and his family were herded into the cellar of their house by a squad of soldiers and there shot and bayoneted to death to the last member—even down to the children's pet spaniel. Later, Bolshevik central authorities arrested twenty-eight of the men involved and executed five of them.

But when the murders occurred, Lenin, Trotsky, and the others had little time to worry about them. Civil war had sprung up all over Russia—it flickered on through the summer of 1918 and into the summer of 1919. In the Urals where the Czechs held out, the Ukraine, the Crimea, Russian Poland, and Finland—everywhere armed resistance to the new Bolshevik government sprang into being. In the case of the Poles and the Finns these were battles for national liberation and were eventually won. In other cases the uprisings were based on many factors—widespread peasant discontent, protest against the Bolshevik dictatorship in Moscow (to which the government had moved from Petrograd early in 1918), simple freebooting by demoralized officers and generals. And the rebellions followed much the same pattern. A general or an admiral would, with Allied financial and supply support (and sometimes French or British troops), set up an independent government and march on Petrograd or Moscow. At first they would encounter warm support among the peasants or perhaps the Cossacks and the conservative socialist leaders. But soon it would emerge that they intended to restore the old czarist regime or one like it, and this support would fall away. Bolshevik agitators would infiltrate their forces, and they would find themselves alone. General Alexei Kaledin, commander of the Cossacks living along the banks of the river Don, committed suicide when he found that his men preferred Bolshevik promises to continued struggle. And the brutality and vengeance the rebellious generals or admirals inflicted on the peasants and workers who fell into their own power turned the masses against them. One after another they collapsed—crushed by the same fact that had made the original Bolshevik triumph all but inevitable: there simply did not exist in Russia any broad class of people who would support a counterrevolution, and the masses were impelled by the logic of their situation to embrace Bolshevism.

The peace conference which ended World War I (and from which the Russians were excluded) pulled the props out from under continued resistance inside Russia when Allied contingents were withdrawn and Russian borders established. The Soviet government saw Russia stripped of many of its captive nations at this conference. Poland, Finland, Latvia, Esthonia, Lithuania received their independence; certain areas of the Ukraine were included in Romania. Nevertheless, the Bolshevik leaders considered themselves well out of it, under the circumstances.

The hero of the civil war years was undoubtedly Trotsky. It was he who made the Red Guard formations into the Red Army, and he who inspired it to become an effective fighting instrument. He would rush from place to place—wherever civil war battles were being fought—in an armored train and he soon established himself as a brilliant military tactician. In the longer view the Bolshevik victory was largely political. The strikes and sabotage of the early months of Bolshevik power were quickly suppressed. And a new political secret police appeared on the scene in the form of the dreaded Cheka. Enemies of the Bolsheviks were arrested and executed ruthlessly by the thousand. A Red terror descended over the country which differed from the revolutionary terror of the French Revolution only in its more thorough and scientific application.

By 1920 peace had been reestablished throughout the Russian land. The Czechs who had involved themselves in Admiral Kolchak's anti-Bolshevik attempts were returned to their newly established country, the Allied troops had been withdrawn, and the Bolsheviks found themselves in supreme power.

The Germans, who had encouraged and welcomed the Bolshevik Revolution, were made to see how short-sighted this policy was. Communist uprisings, directly sparked by the Bolshevik success in Russia, soon broke out throughout Germany and were the deciding factor in her surrender to the Allies and the abdication of the Kaiser. Socialist uprisings in Austria-Hungary helped dissolve that tottering empire in its last days. Lenin and Trotsky had both always insisted that the Russian Revolution could only succeed if revolution broke out in the West. To a certain extent they were proved correct. Although the Communist revolutions in Germany, Hungry, and Austria were brutally suppressed, they nevertheless weakened those countries sufficiently to insure against their intervening in Russian affairs. Likewise, the general war-disillusionment and the rise of the Labour party in England and the Socialists in France guaranteed to the infant Bolshevik state that at least they would not be subjected to invasion. Bolshevik problems in the coming decades were to be largely internal.

While Lenin remained in control, hope for a peaceful and perhaps even democratic solution to Russia's tremendous internal difficulties did not disappear. Even Winston Churchill, one of Lenin's bitterest enemies, conceded: "He alone could have found the way back to the causeway. . . . The Russian people were left floundering in the bog. Their worst misfortune was his birth . . . their next worse, his death." It was in the midst of the most difficult period of Russian recovery, with very many basic problems still undecided, that Lenin met his death. With famine and open peasant revolt inflaming the countryside, with Stalin preparing to seize complete control of the Bolshevik party, with a widespread experiment in limited capitalism (the so-called New Economic Policy) still under way, Lenin in late 1923 suffered a severe brain hemorrhage. On January 21, 1924, he died at the age of fifty-three. Half a century before, Dostoevsky had predicted: "Starting from unlimited liberty it [a Russian revolution] will arrive at unlimited despotism." Although in his life Lenin embodied this prediction, there were few, friends or enemies, who at his death disputed the justice with which the Russian people renamed Petrograd—the city of Peter the Great—Leningrad, the city of Lenin.

If violence and ruthlessness had marked Bolshevik policy during Lenin's lifetime, if the basis for national repression and suffering had been unwittingly laid partly by necessity and partly by misguided fanaticism while he was alive, only after his death did the real storm break. For in those days Stalin, the ultraconservative Bolshevik who had consistently opposed much of Lenin's program, seized control of the Bolshevik (now renamed Communist) party machinery in Russia and, after much ruthless scheming, was able to force Trotsky once again into exile and later to murder nearly all of the Old Bolshevik leaders who had led the revolution.

Stalin's solution to the peasant problem was enforced famine and deportation to Siberia, which cost the lives of untold millions of peasants; his solution to political problems was the murder of all opponents and the setting up of slave labor camps for those who were merely suspected of opposition; his solution to problems of foreign affairs was international espionage, sabotage, and subversion on a vast scale—and finally the ruthless betrayal of anti-Fascist forces throughout Europe by his pact with Hitler. His solution to the problem posed by a brilliant and independent Marxist mind such as Trotsky's was the brutal axe-murder of his rival in Mexico. These charges against the Stalinist regime in Russia are not merely those of its declared

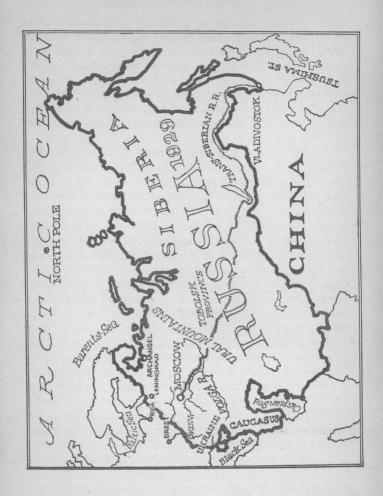

enemies—they are those made by Khrushchev and other Soviet leaders since Stalin's death. These leaders would have us believe that for thirty years Russia was ruled by a man who was growing progressively more and more insane—and there seems no reason to doubt their word. But how did such a man come to power in the new Bolshevik state—and how was he able to retain power with the support of those who later denounced him?

In the days following the revolution *Pravda,* the Bolshevik newspaper, declared: "They wanted us to take the power alone, so that we alone should have to contend with the terrible difficulties confronting the country. . . . So be it! We take the power alone, relying upon the voice of the country. . . . But having taken the power, we will deal with the enemies of the revolution and its saboteurs with an iron hand. They dreamed of a dictatorship of Kornilov. . . . We will give them the dictatorship of the proletariat. . . ." In those harsh words is to be found the core of much that followed. The Bolsheviks, faced with the task of leading a vast, illiterate population on the road to revolution against a fierce and implacable tyranny, had purposely been organized as a small, exclusive, completely dedicated band of leaders. When they triumphed, no machinery existed for, nor was any faith placed in, the transfer of power to the masses they had led. Accustomed to the methods of conspiracy, violence, and discipline, leadership within the party was always certain to fall to the most dominating, the most ruthless. Stalin's rise to power was therefore almost certain.

The Communist party had tradtionally considered itself the head of the industrial working class which would dictate the building of socialism. But in a nation with a small industrial development, in which the overwhelming majority of the population was illiterate, then the

"leadership" of the party was certain to become more
and more despotic, as the rule of a minority always
does. When to this is added the fact that the Russian
people had never experienced democracy or personal
freedom, that their living conditions were such as to
make a mockery of those words, the Communist tyranny of Stalin would seem to have been unavoidable.
The Communists themselves would be the first to point
out that the peculiarities of Stalin's personal madness
were incidental to deeper historic drives. If that was
true, communism in Russia—if it was to follow the
Bolshevik line—was foredoomed to bring with it tyranny and terror. Trotsky always maintained that this
was because the Communist party of Russia abandoned the true tenets of Marxism. But once again, this
was due not to personal whim but to historical impera-
tives.

The Bolshevik Revolution requires justification no
more than the French, English, or American revolution. Revolutions are not conspiracies—they are vast
social upheavals as inevitable and self-justifying as
earthquakes. But the Bolshevik program after the revolution requires justification—just as does any program
of national development—in terms of simple human
happiness. To point to the vast unhappiness of pre-
revolutionary Russia is not enough; human well-being
demands more than merely comparative advances.

EPILOGUE

War and Peace

THE VICTORY OF BOLSHEVISM in Russia did not bring the millennium to that huge and backward country. On the other hand, it must never be forgotten from what depths of ignorance, despair, and cruelty it sprang. Fifteen years after the revolution Trotsky was to write: "Enemies are gleeful that fifteen years after the revolution the soviet country is still but little like a kingdom of universal well-being. Such an argument, if not really to be explained as due to a blinding hostility, could only be dictated by an excessive worship of the magic power of socialist methods. Capitalism required a hundred years to elevate science and technique to the heights and plunge humanity into the hell of war and crisis. To socialism its enemies allow only fifteen years to create and furnish a terrestrial paradise. We took no such obligation upon ourselves. We never set these dates."

Now, almost fifty years after the fall of the Winter Palace, the Union of Soviet Socialist Republics is the second strongest industrial nation on earth. The old jesting about socialist inefficiency came to an end when the first Soviet Sputnik circled the earth. But to ascribe this tremendous industrial advance to socialist methods alone is as incorrect as to ascribe American industrial development solely to capitalist methods. In both countries, geographic and geologic factors were of much more importance than the systems under which they were developed. In both cases continental land masses rich in agricultural, mineral, fuel, and hydro-electric resources had been ruthlessly exploited. Without these resources no gigantic industries would today sprawl around Pittsburgh or Stalingrad, Detroit or Omsk. The productive power of both countries depends less upon their economic systems than upon the natural factors which those systems were able to exploit. The argument as to whether socialism or capitalism is most likely to produce industrial development is thus largely irrelevant.

But what of human happiness? What of freedom, personal liberty? To charges that they are prisoners of their totalitarian state, Russians have replied that we are prisoners of our exploitive economic system. But if that was once true, American history during the past thirty years has proved that, under a democratic political system, tremendous social progress and economic planning are always possible. Recent Russian history, on the other hand, has yet to demonstrate that personal freedom is possible within the rigidly organized Communist social and economic system.

When the world first came to assess the meaning of the Bolshevik Revolution in Russia, it seemed to pose the greatest threat ever raised against Western democratic institutions. European statesmen, at the insistence of their frightened ruling classes, did everything in their power to isolate the new Soviet state. They were not so much afraid in those days of Russian conquest as they were of the appeal communism might make to their own working classes. Only the United States, which did not share in the European heritage of economic privation and rigid class structure, had little realistically to fear from Communist doctrine or propaganda (in spite of politically inspired "Red scares" after both world wars). Yet today the United States finds itself at the head of an armed anti-Communist coalition. Why?

This is not the place to go into the details of recent history which have led to the "cold war." But the most obvious factors in Soviet policy which have contributed to the present state of tension in the world can be briefly stated. Of great importance among these has been the temperament of the Soviet leadership. With the death of Lenin and the Old Bolsheviks, Russian leadership was left largely in the hands of men with little or no personal experience of the world outside Russia. These were men who also still bore the scars of their ruthless and brutal struggle against czarism, poverty, ignorance, and direct foreign intervention in Russian affairs. Suspicion and deep distrust of Western policy, no matter what that policy may be, has often been a decisive factor in Soviet relations with the rest of the world. A second factor of great weight has been the dogmatic devotion of the Soviet government to some outdated doctrines of Marxism. Marx predicted the rapid disintegration of capitalist society as a result of its own inner economic and social "contradictions." Soviet policy, through the financing and planning of subversion, unrest, and class hatred in capitalist nations, has sought to hurry that prediction along. Still another factor which has only recently become clear is the Soviet adoption of some of the expansionist aims of the old czarist regime. Thus, as Soviet strength and industrial power have increased, Russian governments seem to have felt free to indulge in the luxury of playing power politics along Russian borders.

But certainly the most important factor of all in the present hostile relations between Russia and the West has been the Russian internal political system. In a nation in which supreme power passes to politicians ruthless or strong enough to simply grab it (even, as in the case of Stalin, a psychotic personality) and in which the broad masses of the people have no means of restraining that power or even of influencing its decisions, almost anything can happen. Where all policy —and especially foreign policy—is left in the hands and at the whim of a small group of totalitarian leaders, their temptation to solve internal problems by external aggression is always very great. In a world of missiles and H-bombs the spectacle of the immense power of Soviet Russia remaining in the hands of a tiny group of leaders unrestrained by law, responsible only to themselves, and harboring misguided and hostile convictions regarding the rest of the world is frightening indeed.

The United States has met the challenges posed by Soviet policy in a variety of ways. Against Russian expansionist tendencies we have erected a system of armed alliance and today maintain the greatest peacetime military establishment in American history. The deep-rooted mistrust of Western policy on the part of Soviet leaders has been met by a continuing and expanding dialogue in the United Nations and by the greatest possible exposure of Soviet citizens to the realities of life beyond their borders through economic and cultural exchange programs. The Soviet policy of subversion in capitalist nations has been countered with economic aid programs which have undermined the basis of Communist propaganda by dramatically raising the living standards of peoples throughout the world. This in itself has been the best possible demonstration of the irrelevance of Marxist predictions regarding the collapse of capitalist nations.

But to answer the essential and frightening problem posed by the totalitarian structure of Soviet society, there seems little we can do. The problems of political democracy, responsible government, and personal freedom within the Soviet Union can only be solved by the Russian people themselves. Perhaps our greatest contribution toward the solution of these problems will be to continue to expand and give meaning to the political freedom, personal equality, and economic security of *all* our people as an example of what free men working within democratic institutions can accomplish. To face the threat posed by Soviet society in the coming years we will require great fortitude, great wisdom, and— above all—great patience. But we should not be pessimistic about the final outcome.

For if we believe that the overwhelming majority of men everywhere desire peace, personal freedom, and economic security, we must believe that Russians desire these things as much as we do. The final word in the evolution of Soviet society will be spoken, not by a small group of doctrinaire leaders, no matter how apparently powerful, but by the Russian people themselves. If we recall the patience and fortitude with which this people endured an old and seemingly eternal tyranny, and the resourcefulness and courage with which they shattered it, we can remain confident that they will eventually triumph over newer oppressions as they continue to "break a path into the future."

Bibliography

THE RUSSIAN Revolution, although one of the most heavily documented events in history, has aroused and still arouses such violent polemics both for and against that great care must be taken in placing too much reliance on the memoirs of individuals directly involved in the struggle. Thus Trotsky's massive history, the memoirs of Milyukov, the diaries of Sukhanov—while all invaluable primary sources—each reflect the partisanship of their authors. Besides that, the Soviet authorities have been engaged since the early 1920s in a monumental and bald-faced rewriting and suppression of original sources, falsification of documents, and the like, to fit the vagaries

211

of the constantly shifting Party line. A special "suggested reading" list has been provided at the end of the bibliography based on the most readable accounts available, with remarks regarding objectivity.

ABRAMOWITZ, RAPHAEL, *The Soviet Revolution* (New York 1962)

BENEKENDORFF, PAVEL K., *Last Days at Tsarskoe-Tselo;* trans. by M. Baring (London 1927)

BERLIN, ISAIAH, *Karl Marx, His Life and Environment* (New York 1963)

BUCHANAN, SIR GEORGE W., *My Mission to Russia* (New York 1923)

BUNYAN, JAMES, AND FISHER, H. H., *The Bolshevik Revolution, 1917–1918: Documents and Materials* (Stanford 1934)

CARR, EDWARD H., *The Bolshevik Revolution* (New York 1953)

CENTRAL COMMITTEE OF CPSU, *History of the CPSU (B)— Short Course* (Moscow 1952)

CHAMBERLIN, WILLIAM H., *The Russian Revolution, 1917–1921* (New York 1935)

CHERNOV, VICTOR M., *The Great Russian Revolution* (New Haven 1936)

CRESSEY, GEORGE B., *The Basis of Soviet Strength* (New York 1945)

CROSSMAN, RICHARD (ed.), *The God That Failed* (New York 1950)

DENIKIN, ANTON I., *The Russian Turmoil* (London 1922); *The White Army* (London 1930)

DEUTSCHER, ISAAC, *Russia in Transition* (New York 1960)

FISCHER, LOUIS, *The Soviets in World Affairs* (Princeton 1951); *The Life of Lenin* (New York 1964)

FLORINSKY, MICHAEL F., *The End of the Russian Empire* (New Haven 1931)

GOLDER, FRANK A., *Documents of Russian History, 1914–1917*, trans. by E. Aronsberg (New York 1927)

HINDUS, MAURICE G., *The Cossacks* (New York 1945)

HOUGH, RICHARD A., *The Fleet That Had To Die* (New York 1958); *The Potemkin Mutiny* (London 1960)

HRDLICKA, A., *The Peoples of the Soviet Union* (Washington, D.C., 1942)

KENNAN, GEORGE F., *Russia Leaves the War* (Princeton 1956); *Russia and the West Under Lenin and Stalin* (Boston 1960)

KERENSKY, ALEXANDER F., *The Catastrophe* (New York 1927); *Prelude to Bolshevism—The Kornilov Rebellion* (London 1919)

KINDALL, S., *American Soldiers in Siberia* (New York 1945)

KLEINMICHEL, MARIE, *Memoirs of The Countess Kleinmichel;* trans. by Vivian Le Grand (New York 1923)

KORNILOV, A., *Modern Russian History* (New York 1943)

KRASNOFF, GEN. PETER N., *From Double Eagle to Red Flag;* trans. by E. Law-Gisike (New York 1926)

KROPOTKIN, PETER A., *Memoirs of a Revolutionist* (Boston 1899)

KRUPSKAYA, NADIZHDA K., *Memories of Lenin;* trans. by E. Verney (London 1930)

LENIN, VLADIMIR I., *The Revolution of 1917 from the March Revolution to the July Days* (New York 1929); *Collected Works* (International Publishers Edition, New York 1927–1945)

LEVIN, DAVID Y., *The Real Soviet Russia* (New Haven 1945)

LICHTHEIM, G., *Marxism, an Historical and Critical Study* (London 1961)

LIDDELL-HART, BASIL H., *The Red Army* (New York 1956)

LOCKHART, R. H. BRUCE, *Memories of a British Agent* (London 1932)

MARX-ENGELS-LENIN INSTITUTE, *Vladimir Lenin, a Political Biography* (New York 1944)

MARX, KARL, *Capital;* trans. by E. and C. Paul (London 1957)

MAX, ERNEST B., *The Last Episode of the French Revolution* (London 1911)

MAYO, H. B., *Introduction to Marxist Theory* (New York 1962)

The Russian Revolution

MEHRING, FRANZ, *Karl Marx;* trans. by E. Fitzgerald (London 1952)

MILYUKOV, PAUL N., *History of the Second Russian Revolution* (Sofia 1921); *Russia, Today and Tomorrow* (New York 1922)

MIRSKY, D. S., *Russia* (New York 1930)

MOOREHEAD, ALAN, *The Russian Revolution* (New York 1958)

NABAKOFF, CONSTANTINE, *The Ordeal of a Diplomat* (London 1921)

NAZAROFF, A., *The Land of the Russian People* (Philadelphia 1944)

PARES, BERNARD, *The Fall of the Russian Monarchy* (New York 1939); *History of Russia* (New York 1953)

PAYNE, ROBERT, *Marx* (New York 1968)

PLAMENATZ, J. P., *What Is Communism?* (London 1947)

RAUCH, GEORGE VON, *A History of Soviet Russia* (New York 1960)

REED, JOHN, *Ten Days That Shook the World* (New York 1919)

ROCHESTER, A., *Lenin on the Agrarian Question* (New York 1942)

SCHWARZSCHILD, LEOPOLD, *The Red Prussian; The Life and Legend of Karl Marx* (London 1948)

SOROKIN, PITIRIM A., *Leaves From a Russian Diary* (New York 1924); *The Sociology of Revolution* (Philadelphia 1925)

SUKHANOV, NIKOLAI N., *The Russian Revolution;* trans. by J. Carmichael (New York 1955)

TROTSKY, LEON, *My Life; An Attempt at an Autobiography* (New York 1930); *History of the Russian Revolution;* trans. by Max Eastman (New York 1932)

ULAM, ADAM B., *The Unfinished Revolution* (New York 1960)

VERNADSKY, V., *The Russian Revolution, 1917–1921* (New York 1932)

VICO, GIAMBATTISTA, *The New Science;* trans. by Bergin and Fish (New York 1940)

VILLIAMY, C. E., (ed.), *Letters of the Tsar to the Tsaritza, 1914–1917;* trans. by A. L. Hynes (New York 1929)

VYRUBOVA, ANNA A., *Memories of the Russian Court* (New York 1923)

WALLACE, D. MCK., *Russia* (New York 1912)

WHEELER-BENNETT, J. W., *Brest Litovsk, the Forgotten Peace* (New York 1939)

WILLARD, G., *Textes Choisis: François Noël Babeuf* (Paris 1950)

WILLIAMS, ALBERT RHYS, *Through the Russian Revolution* (New York 1921)

WILSON, EDMUND, *To the Finland Station* (New York 1940)

WITTE, SERGEI Y., *Memoirs of Count Witte;* trans. by A. Yarmolinsky (New York 1921)

WOLFE, BERTRAM D., *Three Who Made a Revolution* (New York 1948)

SUGGESTED READING

CROSSMAN, RICHARD (ed.), *The God That Failed* (New York 1950). A collection of essays by former Communists reflecting reasons for their disillusionment.

DENIKIN, ANTON I., *The White Army* (London 1930). Memoirs of the Civil War by one of the defeated anti-Bolshevik commanders.

FISCHER, LOUIS, *The Life of Lenin* (New York 1964). Extremely authoritative and impartial biography.

KOESTLER, ARTHUR, *Darkness at Noon* (New York 1941). Fiction.

KROPOTKIN, PETER A., *Memoirs of a Revolutionist* (Boston 1899). Romantic account of pre-Bolshevik revolutionary activity in the old Empire.

LOCKHART, R. H. BRUCE, *Memories of a British Agent* (London 1932). Blunt and brash account of anti-Bolshevik spying and the escape of Kerensky.

MEHRING, FRANZ, *Karl Marx;* trans. by E. Fitzgerald (London 1952). The classic, impartial biography of Marx.

MOOREHEAD, ALAN, *The Russian Revolution* (New York 1958). A lively account in which much space is devoted to an attempt to prove the Bolsheviks acted as German agents.

WILSON, EDMUND, *To the Finland Station* (New York 1940). A brilliant history of Marxist thought, from Vico to Lenin.

Index

More Outstanding Books By
Robert Goldston

THE LIFE AND DEATH
OF NAZI GERMANY   T404

"Robert Goldston's book is extraordinarily welcome. It splendidly perfoms the task a work of
history should perform . . . I offer the highest
possible praise."
—Peter Gay, *The New York Times Book Review*

THE RISE OF RED CHINA   T410

"A stand-out choice . . . a stunning summation
of the factors that produced modern China."
—*National Catholic Reporter*

"Admirable and intelligent."
—*The New York Times*

THE CIVIL WAR IN SPAIN   T405

"For an introduction to the Spanish Civil War,
its causes, and its results, there is no better book."
—*Chicago Tribune*

These Fawcett Premier Books Are
75¢ Each
Wherever Paperbacks Are Sold